Praise for *Love Without Reason*

"From the moment I met LaRayia, I knew she had a book in her. You could see it in her eyes and in her life. In a world where it can be easy to become complacent, LaRayia shows us how to find our passion again—not just for ourselves, but for others as well. She clearly shows us the power that unconditional love has to change our hearts and the lives of those around us. The radical love you will learn to tap into in this book is not the vapid 'love' so flippantly used today, but a deep, authentic love. This book is a beautiful manual of how to live from that love above all else. A revolutionary manifesto to Love Without Reason."

DR. WILL COLE
leading functional medicine expert and bestselling author
of *The Inflammation Spectrum* and *Ketotarian*

"In these fragmenting times, LaRayia Gaston offers inspiring, tangible awakening tools to get engaged, lean into to giving a f♥ck, and activate micro-gestures of empowered service. *Love Without Reason* is an impassioned call to rise together, transform food scarcity, and nourish our soul's call to be part of the circle of exchange."

SHIVA REA
author of *Tending the Heart Fire* and founder of Global School for Living Yoga

"LaRayia Gaston walks her talk like no other, honey. This woman is 100% LOVE! Reading about her journey will inspire you to celebrate your unique gifts, radiate love, and make a difference in the world."

SAH D'SIMONE
author of *Spiritually Sassy*

"*Love Without Reason* is an empowering yet humbling read that not only reveals why we need to exhibit more love in our life but most importantly how to actually do it. Through personal and relatable stories, LaRayia Gaston makes the complex and daunting concept of doing our part to make the world a better place seem achievable.

Gaston's honesty in describing her journey of integrating the practice of love into her everyday life illustrates how we must strive for progress rather than perfection when making fundamental personal change.

Love Without Reason is an invaluable guidebook to expanding the way we understand love and actualizing the universal good that comes from giving it freely."

ASH BECKHAM
author of *Step Up*

LO
VE

LOVE
WITHOUT
REASON

LOVE

L O

LOVE WITHOUT REASON

THE LOST ART OF GIVING A F♥CK

V E

LARAYIA GASTON

with Christa Bourg

Sounds True
Boulder, CO 80306

Published 2021

Cover design by Rachael Murray
Book design Linsey Dodaro

Printed in the United States of America

Library of Congress Cataloging-in-Publication Data

Names: Gaston, LaRayia, author.
Title: Love without reason : the lost art of giving a f*ck / by LaRayia
    Gaston ; with Christa Bourg.
Description: Boulder, CO : Sounds True, 2021. | Includes bibliographical
    references. | Summary: "In Love without Reason: The Lost Art of Giving a
    F*ck, LaRayia Gaston helps us connect with our hearts, reawaken our
    innate desire to make a difference, and then actually make that
    difference in a way that is both enjoyable and impactful"-- Provided by
    publisher.
Identifiers: LCCN 2020041494 (print) | LCCN 2020041495 (ebook) | ISBN
    9781683646303 (hardback) | ISBN 9781683646310 (ebook)
Subjects: LCSH: Self-actualization (Psychology) | Resilience (Personality
    trait) | Love.
Classification: LCC BF637.S4 G383 2021 (print) | LCC BF637.S4 (ebook) |
    DDC 158.1--dc23
LC record available at https://lccn.loc.gov/2020041494
LC ebook record available at https://lccn.loc.gov/2020041495

10 9 8 7 6 5 4 3 2 1

To my grandmommy, Johnnie Gaston.
I didn't find God in church. I found the Universe through your love.

To my Bodega Baby, Talia, who showed me how important it is to be good
to people while they're here because one day God will ask for them back.

To my father, James Ellis, who chose to be my dad.
You made me believe in the second chances that we're all divinely given,
and you showed me exactly what love could be.

Contents

Introduction

WHY I GIVE A F♥CK

"Life's most persistent and urgent question is,
'What are you doing for others?'"

MARTIN LUTHER KING, JR., *"The Three Dimensions of a Complete Life"*[1]

We all have our own definitions of love that evolve from our unique experiences. Growing up I learned about love from my two moms: the woman I call "mom," who was actually my grandmother, and my birth mom, with whom I no longer have a relationship. Born to a woman who didn't love herself enough to understand how to love others, I spent most of my childhood in a physically and emotionally abusive home.

The experience muddled my idea of what love is, but I was also lucky. My grandmother was the complete opposite of my birth mother in every way that mattered. She saw the good in everyone she met and in every experience she had. She was open, accepting, and so full of love, it was like it spilled out of her. She would visit us often, and I would spend summers with her when I was young. When life became too much for me with my birth mother, I would live with her for stretches of time. What made me so incredibly lucky was having her steady example to counter the one I was learning at home. It's so clear to me now that my life could have turned out very differently if I hadn't been given that gift.

The contrast between my two moms was probably never so stark as when they learned, at different times, that I had a girlfriend.

My birth mom discovered my secret when I had just turned fifteen years old. I hadn't meant for her to find out, but someone saw me kissing my then-girlfriend and told her about it. She came to find me immediately. My best friend, my girlfriend, and I were all hanging out in the living room of my birth mom's house when she rushed in, grabbed me, and pulled me outside. I ended up on the ground in front of the house while she kicked me and called me names, screaming at me, "You're going to hell!" Afterward, I was bleeding so badly I probably should have gone to the hospital, but I didn't want to. Instead, my best friend stayed with me to ice my face. She had watched the whole thing from our living room window, and the experience was so upsetting for her that she was afraid to come out to her own family after that. She, too, was fifteen at the time, and she didn't tell them the truth until more than a decade later, when she was twenty-six years old.

Two years after that, when I was seventeen, I chose to tell my grandmother rather than let her discover it by accident like my birth mother had. My grandmother was born in the 1930s, and I'd always considered her to be pretty conservative because of the way she talked and the way she dressed. She'd also been a faithful churchgoer her entire life, so I was afraid she wouldn't like what I had to say. I didn't think she'd hurt me like my birth mother had—I knew her better than that—but I was afraid she might reject me, which would have been so much worse.

I was sweating I was so nervous, but my grandmother didn't even flinch when I told her. She just looked at me calmly and said, "Do you know how many accounts of homosexuality there are in the Bible?"

"No," I said, afraid of where this was going.

"There are six," she told me. "Do you know how many times the Bible talks about love?"

"No," I said again.

"Me neither," she replied. "It's in there so often that I lost count. It's safe to say that God's emphasis is on love and not on who you're dating."

CHOOSING LOVE

You can imagine how much relief I felt from my grandmother's reaction. She went on to assure me that she would love anyone I loved and that person would always be welcome in her home. And that was it. There was no anger. No drama. Just a pure and simple expression of love.

Somewhere along the way I came to understand that it's our actions, more than our blood relationships, that matter most, and it's our actions that define who we are. My grandmother was the one who acted like a mother in my life, so to me she became my mom.

It was because of these two women that I learned to see love from both sides. From my mom (grandmother), I came to understand love as this infinite and powerful thing that could save people from dark and desperate circumstances. From my birth mother, I learned what a lack of love could do—how living without it could be so corrosive, so destructive.

While I was still living with my birth mother, I would often disappear into books as a way of coping with, or avoiding, the chaos at home. An interest in music drew me to books about Duke Ellington and Miles Davis, which in turn helped me discover a love of biographies. That's how I found Mother Teresa, whose words resonated with me when I was in the third grade, perhaps because I was looking for a way to make sense of my pain: "I have found the paradox, that if you love until it hurts, there can be no more hurt, only more love."[2]

When I became old enough to understand how different my grandmother was from everyone else I knew, I understood that she lived that quote every day. She taught me how to live it too. Her lessons were the reason I started feeding people when I was just fourteen years old. The first person I fed was someone I saw rifling through a trash can behind the restaurant where I worked. The restaurant had closed for the day, and I had the back door open as I was packing up food to be thrown away—perfectly good food, but that's how restaurants operate. I asked the man, "Hey, are you hungry?"

He didn't speak but he nodded at me, so I gave him some food, which he put in his grocery cart. I turned around to grab him a drink, but when I turned back he was already gone.

I was left wishing I could have done more to help. The interaction lasted hardly more than a moment, but it marked the beginning of something for me. After that, every time I saw a displaced person walk by the restaurant, I couldn't look away. I didn't have a lot to give as a teenager, but I would ask if he or she wanted some food. After a while my uncle, who owned the restaurant, found out and forbade me from doing it again. I didn't protest. I just started making food at home and giving that away instead.

One day a few years later, when I was still a teenager, I finally told my grandmother what I'd been doing. She was a faithful tither, giving every Sunday during church services, but I didn't feel like I was getting out of the church experience what she got out of it. So I told her I didn't want to tithe anymore; I wanted to feed people instead.

I'd been thinking about this for a while, but I hadn't told her because I was nervous about disappointing her. My grandmother was always very even-tempered. She never got angry, never raised her voice, but whenever she shook her head at me in disappointment, it always gutted me. I shouldn't have worried in this case because she just looked at me with her typical grace and said: "That's alright. You don't have to give money to the church. That's not what tithing is about. It's about being mindful of others and giving to them what you can. You just have to do your part, whatever that is."

That was all the encouragement I needed. During the years that followed, no matter where I was or what I was doing, I would take time to feed people. I did it quietly, without telling anyone, for more than ten years. I found God in those spaces—not by going to church, but by being of service. In fact, feeding people felt like a religious experience from the very first time I did it. When the man who appeared behind my uncle's restaurant disappeared as quickly as he came, I was left standing there with a startling thought: *That was an angel.* I believed then and I believe now that he showed up in my life at that moment as a sign of what I was meant to do.

Like for many of us, when I first left home and was just starting out in the world, there was a difference between the work I did to make a living and the work I did to give my life purpose. I was a model and an actress, and then I started my own fashion brand, all the while finding time to feed people on the side. That changed in 2016 when I founded Lunch On Me, and my work and my purpose became one. LOM is a nonprofit dedicated to feeding organic, healthy food and offering holistic healing to those experiencing homelessness or hunger. We're based in Los Angeles, so most of our work takes place on or near Skid Row, but so far we've brought our particular brand of love, light, and community to New York, Detroit, Austin, Miami, and Hawaii. With just me, a few employees, and a list of over 900 volunteers, we've gone from serving 500 meals to 10,000 meals a month in less than two years.

Because we insist on as much fresh, organic food as possible, we can't get government funding. (It's too expensive according to government standards, but you'd be surprised how much public money goes toward packaged foods like chips and soda.) Instead, we rely on food donations from grocery stores, restaurants, catering companies, and other businesses. We take their donations and redistribute food that would otherwise go to waste in order to have a positive impact on the environment and the community. With no government help at all, we've gotten our costs down from five dollars per plate to just eighty-nine cents for a generous portion of healthy, organic food.

When people see us on the streets, offering plates of freshly made food to anyone who wants one, they often ask which church we're from. I tell them the truth: we're not affiliated with any church. That confuses a lot of people—sometimes they're even suspicious—and they'll often ask, "Then why are you here?"

Answering that one can be a bit more difficult because we don't have a specific reason—not really. We're not there to save anyone's soul. We're not looking for credit or approval from others. In fact, we don't expect anything in return for what we do. Of course, we often get plenty back for our efforts, but that's not our primary purpose. We show up to serve simply for the sake of it. We believe the world could use more love, and we have love to give. So we give it, just because we can.

That's what it means to Love Without Reason. Over the years, serving people has become my religion, the street my church, and LWR the organizing principle in my life. It's also our rallying call to encourage others to join us.

Not surprisingly, LWR grew out of my grandmother's example. She would do anything to help anybody she could, and she never expected anything in return. She had no debts with anyone because she was *happy* to be of service. She loved to do it. It's who she was. Deep down, I think it's who a lot of us want to be.

There was no reason for my grandmother to give so gladly other than because she believed that's what a person should do. I watched her my whole life, and I came to understand that she was right. It *is* how we should be. The world was better for my grandmother's gifts. The people around her felt valued and cared for. But just as importantly, her own life was full, meaningful, and purposeful up until the day she died. Serving people—or what I call "giving a f♥ck"—was her way of showing love, but also her way of bringing more love into her life. And what I see out there, whether I'm working on Skid Row or speaking in Beverly Hills, is that so many of us are longing for just what she had.

LOVE WITHOUT REASON: A DEFINITION

Being intentional about the act of love, not the outcome. It's love for love's sake and nothing else.

So why do I give a f♥ck? Because I don't have a choice. It's like asking why we love. We love because it's who we are. It's in our nature. It's what our souls long to do. So why not give our souls more of what they want?

SO WHAT'S THIS BOOK ABOUT, ANYWAY?

When I tell you that I've met so many people out there longing for the kind of love that my grandmother embodied, I'm not just talking about the people

I meet on Skid Row or in other underserved communities throughout the country. I'm talking about the hundreds and hundreds of people who show up to volunteer for LOM and the tens of thousands more who follow us on social media. I'm talking about the thousands of people I speak to at wellness conferences and community events each year who are searching for something more. I'm talking about all the nonprofit workers, social workers, teachers, parents, and others I've met who help people through what they do but who don't always feel satisfied or sustained by it. And I'm talking about you.

What I see over and over again is that so many people out there, no matter what their level of privilege, wish that the world were a better place. They want there to be less fighting and less hate. They wish they didn't have to witness so much suffering. They want to make a difference, and they want that difference to matter. They want all of this, but they don't know how to have it. They want all of this, but they don't even know if it's possible. Many of them already believe that it isn't, so they don't even try.

But what if it *is* possible? What if it's possible to feel a little better about the world and our place in it? Almost everyone I've ever talked to about this, almost everyone I've ever met, will say, "Yes, I want that!" The question is *how*?

I don't know where you went to high school, but where I went there wasn't a course on "Making a Difference in the World" or "How to Do Your Part." The world isn't typically organized to teach us these skills or even provide us with the inspiration to learn them ourselves. What we need is a way to bear witness to all the many things that have gone wrong in the world, and then—instead of shutting down or turning away because it all feels like too much—empower ourselves to give a f♥ck.

So that's what this book is: a course on "Giving a F♥ck 101." A blueprint that will show, step by step, how we can each build a better world around us—what we can do, how we can do it, and how we can strengthen our hearts so we're up to the challenge. Our giving instinct is like a muscle. If we don't use it, we will

WHY I GIVE A F♥CK . . .

"I feel like we can do better together than we can separated and apart. I feel like there's unity in love, and if everybody could just tap into the good in them, we could all be like Power Rangers. I'm not messing around when I say that. If we all tapped into our inner powers and came together, we could do so much more to make this world better. This world is ours, and if we could just do that, can you imagine how amazing the world could be?"

JAMILA
nurse, age 32

lose it—and for some of us, it may already be weakened from disuse. But if we exercise it regularly, we can make it strong and resilient again. Let's not forget that our hearts are muscles too, and they're looking to us to make good use of them. And because the heart is a muscle that gets stronger with practice, I've included what I call "heartwork" exercises throughout the book to help you build its strength and capacity.

And even beyond the how, we'll talk about the why—why we need to learn this, for our own sake as well as each other's. It's not our fault the world is the way it is, but we are suffering because of it. And wouldn't we all like to suffer a little less? Don't we all wonder sometimes if there isn't more to life than this? We have to wonder what it's costing us to turn our backs on the possibility that things could be better. We have to wonder what it's doing to us—to our happiness, to our hearts, to our sense of power and agency, to our sense of self—to deny the natural giving and loving parts of ourselves because it just feels too hard or too painful to use them freely in this mixed-up world.

"I found the paradox, that if you love until it hurts, there can be no more hurt, only more love"—that's what Mother Teresa said, and I believe it. It's also the mission of this book: to help us all open up our experience of love so that we are able to give more of it, in more places, to more people, for more reasons—or even for no reason at all. Because imagine what the world would be like, imagine what *we* would be like, if we could only do that for ourselves and for each other. Wouldn't that be something to see?

Besides, there's a natural high that comes from giving and loving, and who doesn't want to feel better? And besides that besides, why not just try Loving Without Reason? What do you have to lose anyway?

1

HOW GIVING A F♥CK
CAN CHANGE YOUR LIFE

*"When we love, we always strive to become better than
we are. When we strive to become better than we are,
everything around us becomes better too."*

PAULO COELHO, *The Alchemist*[1]

Raise your hand if you think the world as it exists right now is just plain great. You wouldn't change a thing. Practically perfect in every way that you can think of.

Not raising your hand? I didn't think so. Me neither.

Pick a problem, any problem—poverty, disease, inequality, violence, the climate crisis, political crisis, economic crisis, housing crisis. Pick any one of them, or even all of them at once, and ask yourself: How did the world get this way?

Yeah, I don't know either. But I'll tell you one thing that I do know for sure: the world didn't get this way because we all cared too much.

I believe that we have a "giving a f♥ck" problem in our culture. I first noticed it in my twenties when I started volunteering at different nonprofits around Skid Row, an area of downtown Los Angeles that's home to one of the nation's largest concentrations of people living on the streets. It was an eye-opening experience, and not for the reasons you might expect.

I had chosen the work because I wanted to connect with people, learn their stories, and build relationships so I could be of better service. I think the same intention drove most of us working there, at least in the beginning. But the reality of the work was something very different.

One of the foundations where I volunteered occupied seven floors in the heart of Skid Row, only one of which was dedicated as a shelter for the displaced. The rest of the floors were offices or empty space, which could have been used to expand the foundation's programs but wasn't for reasons that were never explained. Then there was the director, who drove a Tesla and wore expensive suits when he showed up to work—on Skid Row. He would attend the organization's fancy fundraisers but never interacted with the people we served. The worst part was that no matter how much money the foundation had—and it had a lot for a nonprofit—workers were constantly being asked to find new ways to cut corners, not in administrative costs, but in the services offered to the people we were meant to be helping.

One day, the director decided to save money by canceling a graduation ceremony for a group completing a drug rehab program. The organization had just secured yet another multimillion-dollar grant, so they could afford the relatively small cost of the celebration, but the director still considered it an unnecessary expense. Now, getting sober is hard. Getting sober while you're living on the streets is practically heroic, so I couldn't believe he'd outright cancel something the graduates had worked so hard for. Some of them, in their entire lives, had never had even a birthday party thrown in their honor, so this celebration was a big deal. It was something they'd been looking forward to, and here we were going to take it away from them at a pivotal moment when they were trying to make big changes in their lives.

It just felt wrong, so I decided to throw the party myself. I bought food for about fifty people and cooked it in my kitchen at home. I made the kinds of things I would make for friends and family if they were coming over for a special dinner—shrimp pasta, salmon with garlic, herbed rice, and fresh green salad. It didn't even cost that much, but the reaction was something I'll never forget.

I didn't know at the time that people on Skid Row don't get a lot of fresh food. Practically every person who came to get a plate said something about how grateful they were to have a real, home-cooked meal. Pretty soon a few approached hesitantly to ask for more. When I said, "Yes, of course," it started a wave, and everyone was asking for seconds, then thirds. I just stood there serving plate after plate, swallowing back tears. It was the first time I'd cooked for so many people, and I'd been stressing about it the entire time I was preparing the food. At the same time, it had felt like such a small gesture considering what these graduates had accomplished. But all that receded in the face of what I was witnessing: person after person finding such joy in my simple gesture and reflecting that joy back to me by offering their heartfelt thanks for what I'd given them.

Not long after, I decided I could do a better job on my own of fostering that kind of joy. I stopped volunteering for other organizations and started Lunch On Me. I'd never run a nonprofit before, so I never could have imagined we'd grow so fast or get so much attention for our work. I attribute it to the fact that I tapped into a need almost by accident.

Here's the thing: I'm not talking about the needs of people on Skid Row or the other displaced people we serve. That's the kind of need I've long understood. It was the needs of our volunteers, partners, sponsors, and champions that, as time went on, really surprised me.

On the day of the graduation ceremony, my focus was on the graduates and on celebrating their accomplishments, but since then I've given more thought to the people who worked alongside me at the nonprofit. They surely didn't go into this kind of work for the money. After all, many of us were volunteers, and the professionals among us didn't get paid well enough to be attracted by dollar signs. They had to be drawn to the work because they wanted to help people and make a difference. You can imagine, then, what it must have felt like to be in a position where you could really impact someone, where you could make their day by just throwing a modest party, and then be told that it wasn't worth the trouble. Working at that nonprofit taught me a valuable lesson, which is that putting our hands in our pockets when we know we could be reaching out to someone, doing little to nothing when we know we could be doing something good and purposeful, that holding ourselves back in this way makes a person feel like crap.

Unfortunately, I was the only one that day who openly questioned whether canceling the party was the right thing to do. Even after I took responsibility for it, no one offered to help me. I don't think it was because they were bad people. I think they had just grown accustomed to a culture that doesn't prioritize things like serving and caring over profits, even in the world of nonprofits, where helping people is supposed to be the main purpose. I think this is a common problem among people in "helping" professions. Most people choose to become something like a nurse, social worker, or nonprofit worker because they want to make a difference in people's lives, but the structures in place don't always support that intention. Instead, people learn to deny the part of themselves that longed to really serve people. In the case of the organization I was working with, it was like everyone there had gone numb.

In contrast, at Lunch On Me we rely on the help of a revolving roster of volunteers for all our services and events, and the sense of satisfaction that I see regularly on their faces is like day to my former coworkers' night. Our volunteers aren't getting paid and most of them have careers in completely separate fields, but they come anyway. And they keep coming back. I believe it's because we don't ask them to sit in cubicles and stuff envelopes. We don't ask them to stand on a street corner with a clipboard asking for money. We ask them to connect with someone in need and offer whatever they can to help—whether it's a plate of food, some company, a compliment, a sympathetic ear, a hug, or all of the above and more. And when they do something that causes a smile to dawn on someone's face, it's reflected on their own. Giving and spreading love is contagious, and that's what makes them so *happy* to volunteer.

I see it every day: there are so many people out there longing for an opportunity to do good, to make a difference, to connect with people, and to be of service if only for an hour or two. There are so many people out there longing for an opportunity to give a f♥ck. They want to be conduits for giving, sharing, helping, caring—for love—and when they get a chance, the effect can be pretty profound.

THE LONELY, NARCISSISTIC, DEPRESSED, AND ANXIOUS WORLD WE LIVE IN

One of the biggest barriers to giving a f♥ck is that our culture is set up to reinforce our separateness rather than our connectedness or coming together. Even if we don't mean to, it's far too easy to end up living in our own bubbles. In the 2016 presidential election, for example, polling by *The Washington Post* showed that large groups of Hillary Clinton voters didn't know anyone voting for Donald Trump, and vice versa.[2] And that's just politics. Despite the ideal of America as a melting pot, the neighborhoods where we live and spend most of our time are not all that diverse.

We often think of diversity in terms of race. While it's true that most American neighborhoods lack that kind of diversity, even the ones that have it tend to be sorted in other ways. Most of us live and interact with people who are pretty similar to us in terms of economics, education, beliefs, and professional categories like white collar versus working class.[3]

At the same time, we're not encouraged to spend a lot of time looking outside our bubbles and beyond our own experiences. Many of the tools we use today to "connect" us have ended up fostering a kind of stagnation, even narcissism. On social media, we associate most often with like-minded individuals, and then the platforms feed us more of the same. Any casual stroll through Instagram or Facebook will show that the selfie far outnumbers the group photo these days. Platforms like Twitter too often feel like places where people go to vent their frustrations rather than seek common ground. The Internet in general and social media specifically provide lots of opportunities to showcase our accomplishments, possessions, thoughts, feelings, complaints, even what we had for dinner from the comfort and safety of our living rooms, but not to get out and connect in person as we once did.

In our siloed, me-centric culture, it probably comes as no surprise that researchers have found that empathy is on the decline. A study by the University of Michigan Institute for Social Research reported that, beginning in the year 2000, college-age people in the US exhibited lower levels of empathy compared to the same group in earlier generations.[4] Depression and anxiety are also on the rise in this country, with the rates among teens and young adults rising the fastest.[5] One has to wonder if there isn't a connection. The less we care, and the less we feel cared for, the more anxious and depressed we become.

At the same time that we're feeling more anxious and depressed, and less empathetic toward one another, we have access to so much information about the sheer number and magnitude of the problems our society faces. If we're not myopically focused on our own lives, we can become so busy worrying about the latest national or international headlines that we lose track of what's happening in our own homes and communities. So many of us don't talk to our neighbors anymore. We may not even know what's truly going on with our friends. Because of this, we're so rarely in a position to be of real service to the people around us.

It's pretty clear to me, and probably to you too if you think about it, that our society is suffering. But I also want us to think about what's happening to us as individuals. I believe we're losing sight of each other and our shared humanity, and it's taking its toll on us mind, body, and soul. We're losing our ability to give a f♥ck, and it may literally be killing us.

That's not an exaggeration. Just recently, global healthcare giant Cigna decided it was time to study something that isn't talked about much in terms of its impact on our health: loneliness. Their survey results suggested that not only are *most* Americans lonely (as measured on what's called the UCLA Loneliness Scale), the younger you are, the more likely you are to suffer from loneliness. According to Douglas Nemecek, MD, a chief medical officer at Cigna, "Loneliness has the same impact on mortality as smoking fifteen cigarettes a day, making it even more dangerous than obesity."[6]

That just goes to show you the damage a lack of connection can do. But this isn't a book about our health. This is a book about our souls—our individual souls and our collective soul. Many of us have forgotten what it feels like to give to someone who isn't in our immediate family—not for status, money, recognition, tax breaks, or anything other than because we can and we want to. Next time you have a chance, visit your local playground and watch the little kids playing in the sandbox. They naturally strike up instant relationships, share space, trade snacks, and give and take toys. They do these things not to be "good" or to get credit for them, and not because they're obliged to. They do them because it feels right. They do them because it's a natural part of what makes us human. We have to ask ourselves: What is it doing to us to deny that part of ourselves?

THERE IS ANOTHER WAY

Wouldn't it be nice to be like those kids in the sandbox again? To share with one another more easily and to coexist more peaceably. To have more of those moments when you unexpectedly connect with someone on the subway or bus. Or when you offer someone a compliment and you can just tell it was exactly what the person needed to hear. Or when you're in line for your morning coffee and get a chance to make someone's day by buying him or her a cup too—which then makes your day in return. I think we need to start from a simple place. We need to start by telling ourselves that the world can be better than this, and that we can play a part in making it better. We can make it better because we are a part of the world, and *we* can be better than this.

Believing that may require a bit of faith, but I don't think it's really that much of a stretch. If you think about it, if you look around, I bet you'll find that you already believe it. You have almost surely witnessed some instance or some place where a person gave freely and the positive effect it had on others.

For me, that place was my grandmother's house in Arizona. Because her heart was always open, her house was always full. It was such a contrast to the life I'd had with my birth mother on the East Coast.

My grandmother had a basic brick, ranch-style house in the desert, about forty-five minutes from the Mexican border. Coming from the city, it felt like the middle of nowhere to me, and yet people were always appearing, as if out of nowhere, to gather under the massive orange tree in her backyard or assemble around her dining room table. Neighbors, friends, family members, acquaintances she'd met only that day—her door was open to anyone, and in my mind I picture her always cooking so that she'd have something to serve to whomever showed up. Of course, when you eat with people, you get to know them, so she was always lending her support and helping to solve problems. She'd look after people's kids, loan them money, give them a place to stay when they needed one. She was free with her kind words and wise counsel, and people felt welcome in her home no matter what. In my memory, her house remains the safest place I've ever known.

My grandmother was just one woman, and yet she created that kind of space for me and for a whole community of people. Imagine what the world would be like if it were populated with people like her.

❤ HEARTWORK ❤

Think about the people in your life, past or present, that you consider to be the most caring, the most generous, and the most loving. Write down their names and a little bit about what makes you feel this way about them. Recall any memories when you personally felt cared for and loved by them.

GETTING OUT OF YOUR BUBBLE

It's probably because of these early experiences that feeding people became my thing. I saw how food brought people together and fed their souls as well as their stomachs. I've always fed people, but it became a profession only when I moved to Los Angeles, where homelessness is such a massive problem, one that the *Los Angeles Times* called "a national disgrace" after the number of chronically homeless people in the county topped 57,000.[7]

If you're sitting in your living room reading about this issue in the newspaper, it's easy to feel overwhelmed. Hundreds of millions of dollars have been spent on the problem in recent years, and the numbers have only gotten worse. It's enough to make a person want to give up without even trying. It's hard enough to make our own lives work. How can we possibly have anything left over to give? And to what end, if all the government's resources can't even make a dent?

But that's the view from your living room. When you get out there and connect with people one on one, the feeling is very different. I never feel depressed or overwhelmed by the problem because I don't try to solve it. Instead, I get out there and meet people. I open my heart to them and offer what I have to give. I don't try to make a difference in Los Angeles's "homeless problem"; I go out and try to make a difference in the life of Kevin, or Ms. Brenda, or Scotty, or Janet, just for today. And I do. I know I do, because I see it and I feel it. And it's a really good feeling.

It's a feeling that's too often absent from our day-to-day lives but doesn't have to be. You can feel it too if you open yourself up to it. Feeding and caring for the displaced is what I've chosen to give a f♥ck about, but it's important to keep in mind that you can do you. Maybe you want to connect with foster children or seniors. Maybe you're drawn to support the ill or infirm. Maybe your neighborhood school could use some help, or even just your neighbor next door. We'll talk more about this idea in a later chapter, but for now it's important to understand that it doesn't matter so much what you give or to whom; it just matters that you get out of your bubble and reach out to someone new. It just matters that you get into the habit of giving.

And when you do, you'll discover that you no longer need to ask the question of how you'll ever have something left over to give in your busy, overburdened, overstressed life. That's because you'll find that giving doesn't deplete us. It makes us stronger, fuller, more energized, and more capable. I talked in the introduction about Mother Teresa's paradox, and I believe I've discovered one of my own: the more we give, the more able we are to give even more.

WHY YOU NEED TO GIVE GIVING A CHANCE

Loving Without Reason can be hard sometimes, and there are lots of reasons not to give a f♥ck. Right now, despite all that I've been talking about, in the back of your mind you may be thinking about all the things that can get in the way. I get it. I've heard all the reasons why not, and I'm not discounting them. In fact, we'll spend a good amount of time in the next chapter addressing them directly. So hold on to those "why nots" for just a moment, because first we need to talk about what happens when we don't give giving a chance.

In 2018, I started working on a documentary about what life is like on Skid Row. I decided if I really wanted to tell the story, I needed to experience what it's like to live like the people I serve every week. I got myself a tent and set it up next to the tent of my friend, Ms. Brenda, who is in her sixties and has lived on Skid Row for twelve years. Then I did what she does. I slept on the ground every night. I wore the same clothes day after day. I ate what she ate. I went to the bathroom where she goes to the bathroom. And when I needed something, I went out and begged for the money to buy it.

I'd been there about two weeks when the weather report said that heavy rain was coming. Before starting this project, I'd given a lot of thought to the different problems, even dangers, I might encounter while living on the streets. Unfortunately, weather hadn't been one of them. After all, this is Los Angeles we're talking about, so the possibility of rain hadn't even crossed my mind. I was completely unprepared, so I consulted my friends on Skid Row: "What do you do here when it rains?"

Tarps were the answer. My tent wasn't going to be enough to keep out a hard rain, and there wasn't enough space in the local shelters to accommodate everyone. I needed a couple tarps to shore up my tent and keep myself dry. Because if I got wet, I would be cold and miserable for as long as the rains lasted.

Of course, tarps cost money, and I hadn't brought any with me. Not a lot of money as it turned out—$24 was the cost of two tarps—so I decided to do what any other person on Skid Row would do in this situation: I would panhandle. Surely I could make at least that much over the course of the day if I set my mind to it. Skid Row, after all, is surrounded by a well-trafficked area with lots of businesses and mid- to upper-income residences. I was certain I could get what I needed.

I set up outside of Gold's Gym and placed beside me a small box on which I'd written: Love Without Reason. I approached everyone I could, tried to tell them why I needed the money, and asked for their help.

Five to six hundred people passed by me without offering a penny. I was getting more and more frustrated by the hour, more and more tired of asking people for help only to be ignored. The amount of rejection I experienced over the course of one afternoon was more than I was used to bearing, and I've borne my fair share.

It was late afternoon and I was sitting against the wall with my empty box beside me, my head resting on my knees, when I finally heard something that lifted my spirits: the sound of change dropping into my box. I looked up on the verge of tears, ready to express my heartfelt thanks, not just for the money, but for restoring my faith in humanity. I wanted to believe that in this world of excess, no real need would go unmet if a person was only willing to humble herself and ask.

What I saw when I raised my head gutted me. The person who finally stopped after so many had ignored me, the person who finally cared enough to share his change with me, that person was a homeless man.

I was so stunned that I wasn't able to say thank you, and the man started to walk away. My friend Nema, who'd been filming me all week for the documentary, had been watching from a discreet distance. He jumped up and followed the man, stopping him to ask why he'd chosen to help.

"Because I've been there before," the man responded. When I caught up to them, he turned to me and gave me a hug. "It's gonna be okay," he said reassuringly.

I told him how grateful I was to him and also why I had to return his money. I couldn't take it knowing he needed it more than I did. I went back to panhandling, and only one other person that day gave me money. Amazingly, he turned out to be homeless too.

Something changed in me after that. The idea that the only two people willing to help were the ones who had almost nothing themselves really shook me. I'd been feeding people for fifteen years at that point. I'd been working on Skid Row for the past two. I'd seen plenty over that time, but it had never occurred to me that things were really that bleak.

And I don't mean bleak for the people of Skid Row. I mean bleak for all of us. How did we get to a point where so many of us walk through our lives with such dark blinders on? How did we get to the point where we're able to walk past people's suffering as if it were nothing? As if they deserved what they've got when we don't even know who they are.

I realized something that day. I think I've always known it in my heart, but it took that experience for me to be able to articulate it: We need to change. We need to start showing up in our lives in a different way. If not for the sake of our families and the people around us; if not for the sake of our neighborhoods, our communities, our country, our world; if not for all that, then for ourselves. We have to ask ourselves: If we've grown accustomed to those blinders that keep us separated from one another, then what has that done to our souls?

I never did get enough money for even one tarp. (Thankfully it didn't rain for more than a day, but I spent one long, soggy night in my soaked tent.) But when I speak in front of audiences these days, I often tell that story. I tell it to them as a challenge. I tell them there are people out there praying for things that they could give so easily. They are praying for the pocket change you might lose in the washer without noticing. They are praying for the acknowledgment you could give by simply saying hello when you pass them on the street. They are praying that someone will listen to their story. They are praying for a chance to matter. So many of us feel disempowered in our lives, but maybe that's because we're not seeing all the ways we could be making a difference.

GIVING A F♥CK IS A CHOICE

I believe we all have more choices than we realize. Whether or not we're going to make a positive difference in the world is a choice—one we're presented with daily. We all need to take stock because *we* are the problem. Not just the government, the media, the other political party, or the people who live on the other side of the tracks, but us. There are so many times when we could help, but we don't. We have the resources, but we don't use them well. We have the ability, but we don't have the will. We have to ask ourselves: Why not? What's gone wrong? Why don't we care enough about each other? And if we don't care about each other, what kind of people are we?

When I go down to Skid Row every week, an area that's walking distance from my home, it's hard not to see it as a microcosm of everything that's gone wrong in our society. Sure, there are people there who need food, jobs, homes—things that most of you reading this book will have. They need these things, but what they also need is healing. They need to feel seen and heard, validated and important. They need an escape from life's stresses, a way to tamp down the everyday pressures. They need security, safety, moments of peace. They need to feel connected to others. They need support. They need love.

Isn't that what we all need? We need to start asking ourselves if we're happy with the way things are. With how our lives are turning out. With the quality of our relationships. With how we're contributing to our communities and what we're putting into the world. Not just whether we're okay with it or whether we're comfortable with who and where we are, but whether we're really, truly, fully *happy*.

And if we're not happy, then perhaps it's also time to ask whether we're getting in our own way. We so desperately need to empower the concepts of caring and love, instead of "not giving a f♥ck," for a whole lot of reasons. Because it feels like things are going off the rails in our culture. Because it feels like so many people are being left out. Because we want to leave a better world for the next generation. But if we want just one simple reason, consider this: we'll start getting what we need from this world when we learn how to give it.

We are an increasingly lonely, disconnected, apathetic, anxious, depressed society. That's not my interpretation—that's what the research says. Even life expectancy is on the decline in the United States for the first time in twenty-five years.[8] The symptoms of a massive "giving a f♥ck" problem are all around us, and they appear to be getting worse.

We are still the richest country in the world, but we have to be doing something wrong if this is the state of things despite all our advantages. So I'm proposing we try something new and maybe a little bit radical. I propose we try giving a f♥ck for a change. And not just GAF, but GAF in the extreme. GAF without fear. GAF without prejudice. GAF without worrying that we won't have enough or that we'll make a mistake or that someone won't appreciate it or that what we give will be wasted. I propose that we give a f♥ck because we have love inside us that longs to be expressed, and GAF can be our way of expressing that love.

Does that sound like a lot? Don't worry, we have the rest of this book to talk about how it can be done. For now, let's just focus on the intention. We all want this to be a better world, don't we? So instead of getting angry about it and complaining on social media, instead of hiding ourselves away in despair, let's just admit to ourselves that we want things to change and then resolve to do something about it. I'm not going to ask you to save the world, certainly not all by yourself. All you need to do is brighten your little corner of it. And then together, we can bring the light.

♥ HEARTWORK ♥

We all want this world to be a little bit different, a little bit better, in one way or another. If that's what we want, we need to start looking at how we can contribute to the change.

When I want something to be different in my life, I make a point of keeping it top of mind. One of my favorite tactics is to put sticky notes on my bathroom mirror. I choose the mirror because I know that I look at it regularly—a couple times a day at least—so it's a good place for reminders about what I want for my life.

To change something or accomplish something new, I'll use two sticky notes. On the first I'll write what I want to happen. On the second I'll write what I'm willing to do or give up to get it.

For example, if you've realized that you have a habit of holding onto things, you might write:

1) I want to become a forgiving person.

2) I'm willing to let go of my need to be right and practice listening more and reacting less; I'm willing to be the bigger person and to reach out first during conflicts.

Or, if you want to open your own business, you might write something similar to what I wrote when I started my clothing brand years ago:

1) I want to work for myself and launch my own clothing brand.

2) I'm willing to give up the security of a 9-to-5, put in extra hours, use some of my savings, and even give up sleep if necessary to make it happen. I'm willing to work on expanding my capacity to trust myself and to trust in a Universe that will provide a path for me if I only look for opportunities.

2

START WITH A RESET

*"Seek not to change the world, but choose to
change your mind about the world."*

FOUNDATION FOR INNER PEACE, *A Course in Miracles[1]*

I f we can learn how to really give a f♥ck about others, not only can we have a better world, but we can lead healthier, happier, more purposeful lives. So what's getting in our way? Or, for some of us, we may need to ask: How can we get out of our own way so we can start helping others?

GAF doesn't have to be all that hard, but it may require us to do some things a little differently than we're used to. That means we're going to have to reset ourselves a bit in terms of our mindset, or our default way of thinking. We can do this by cultivating just three basic qualities, or what I call the three Be's. You need to know how to:

1) Be mindful

2) Be intentional

3) Be generous

We'll cover each of these in turn over the course of this book, but in this chapter we'll focus on shifting our mindset to a more giving and loving—and also truer—place through mindfulness.

That's how we plant the seeds, and then what we water will grow.

MINDFULNESS

Our mindset affects our behavior, even (or especially) when that behavior is habitual yet doesn't make a lot of sense. Mindfulness allows us to become more aware of how we think so that we can reset, first our mindset, and then our actions when they don't serve us or others. This isn't about policing our thoughts. It's about avoiding the trap of doing without thinking, reacting without understanding. Because if we don't understand what we're doing and why, then how can we expect to make things different?

I was once in line at a coffee shop, minding my own business, when a bus pulled up outside. Off hopped two kids of about fourteen years old who came inside and stood in line behind me. When it was my turn, I placed my order and stepped aside to wait for my coffee, which gave me a front-row seat for what happened next.

The two kids, both boys, were the awkward and uncomfortable type. I could see immediately that they were the kind of kids who don't like to draw too much attention to themselves, trying instead to make themselves quiet and small so they can hide in plain sight—probably because the world hasn't been all that kind or accepting toward them during their short lives. When it was their turn at the head of the line, one of them stepped forward shyly and whispered to the barista, "May I have some water?"

"Water is for customers ONLY," the barista replied loudly enough for everyone in the small coffee shop to hear. A few gazes turned, and the boys hung their heads in embarrassment. Neither said anything in reply, and instead they turned around to leave.

I stopped them before they could go and looked at the barista, who was still smirking at the boys as if they were worthless peasants who had trespassed in his coffee kingdom.

"You have to be living paycheck to paycheck if you're working here," I said to him. "Your circumstances can't be that far away from these boys'. I bet the company you work for would replace you in a minute if it could find someone to do your job for just one dollar less an hour, and then you might be the one asking a stranger for something you needed. But right now, you're lucky enough to be in a position where you could give these kids something they need that no one will even miss. You're going to give them some water, and you're going to give it to them in the *large* cups."

I then turned to the boys and asked them if they wanted anything else. They were smiling just a little to themselves, but they said, "No, just the water."

The barista was the one who was quiet now. As he turned around to get their water, I said to the boys, "Don't ever be afraid to ask for what you want. You may not always get it, but closed mouths never get fed." They thanked me, took their water, and left, holding their heads just a little bit higher than before.

Some people might think I was too harsh with that barista, but I don't think I was any harsher with him than he was with those boys. I also think we all need opportunities to examine why we act the way we do. That barista was given a chance to help. Not only to help, but to help a couple of kids. Not only that, but to help in a way that would have cost almost nothing in terms of time, effort, or money. And yet, he chose to say no and to do it in a way that embarrassed the kids for asking. Why?

When I talk about mindfulness, this is what I mean: we all need to be asking ourselves more questions about why we do what we do and why we don't give more often. Why do we choose to respond in a certain way? What makes us choose not to help someone when we're presented with an opportunity? Why are we willing to help some people and not others? And, in the barista's case, what made him decide that two young, quiet, respectful kids deserved to be shamed and were undeserving of a simple cup of water?

I don't think the barista meant to be cruel or callous. My guess is he wasn't thinking about what he was doing at all. Maybe he was having a bad day. Maybe he hadn't been treated all that well himself by the people he worked for or the customers he dealt with. Maybe he had been hurt, diminished, and embarrassed in his own life, and then he instinctively turned those negative feelings toward the only people around who had less power than he did. I can understand that and even feel sympathy for it, but it doesn't mean I accept it.

We can do better. We need to do better. There are some default ways in which many of us think about people, think about giving, and think about love that need to be examined. We all walk through life with certain assumptions that guide our behavior. In other words, we all have stories we tell ourselves, but we don't have to take them as givens. That's where mindfulness comes in. Instead of taking something as a given, we can ask ourselves: Are the stories we tell ourselves true? Are they supporting the kind of world we want to live in and the way in which we want to show up in that world?

"You often say, 'I would give, but only to the
         deserving.'
The trees in your orchard say not so, nor the flocks in
         your pasture. They give that they may live, for to
         withhold is to perish.
Surely he who is worthy to receive his days and his
         nights, is worthy of all else from you.
And he who has deserved to drink from the ocean
         of life deserves to fill his cup from your little
         stream.
And what desert greater shall there be, than that
         which lies in the courage and the confidence, nay
         the charity, of receiving?
And who are you that men should rend their bosom
         and unveil their pride, that you may see their
         worth naked and their pride unabashed?
See first that you yourself deserve to be a giver, and
         an instrument of giving.
For in truth it is life that gives unto life—while you,
         who deem yourself a giver, are but a witness."

KHALIL GIBRAN, *The Prophet*[2]

MONEY MONEY MONEY

So many people hate to talk about money, but it's a topic that's too important to ignore. In this chapter, we're going to talk through a number of tricky topics that we could all benefit from bringing more mindfulness to, but I want to start with our relationship with money because it's such an integral part of our lives. After all, we live in a capitalist society, a consumerist culture, and it's something that affects our thinking and our choices whether we want it to or not.

As the founder of a nonprofit, I have to talk about money all the time. I have to ask people to give money, or to give their goods or time, which are worth money. What I've found is that almost everyone falls into one of two mindsets when it comes to this subject: they either approach money from an attitude of scarcity or an attitude of abundance.

The difference boils down to this: either people are afraid they'll never have enough, or they believe that the world will provide for them if they just look for opportunities. Of course, the attitude a person adopts has little to do with how much that person has. Some of the richest people in the world operate from an attitude of scarcity, as do some of the richest countries.

There are a couple of problems that I frequently see in people operating from an attitude of scarcity. First is that it's often not a particularly logical or consistent point of view. For example, I have people tell me that they can't give to others because they can't spare what they have, or because they worry that if they give it away now, then they won't have enough for themselves in the future. Here's where we have to look closely at the stories we tell ourselves because I simply don't think that makes a lot of sense. I'm not going to ask anyone to put themselves in the poorhouse in order to give to others, but can any of us really say that we have *nothing* left over to give after we fulfill our own basic needs? No extra time or money or goods that we can spare? If you really do feel that way, you might want to take a hard look at how much we all typically waste on a regular basis, probably without even thinking much about it.

In the US, for example, about one in nine Americans was food insecure in 2018, including more than 11 million children, and yet thirty to forty percent of our food supply goes uneaten.[3] Food waste is the number one material sent to landfills, and guess where most of it comes from? Not from farms or stores or restaurants. It comes from us—from our own households.[4] That means your typical American adult buys more food than she or he can eat and ends up throwing a portion of it away on a regular basis. If we could find a way to redistribute all the food that goes to waste in this country, then no one would need to go hungry. Think about that: It's not a matter of having too little food for everyone in the country to eat. It's that we don't care enough to get what we already have to the people who need it.

There's clearly a disconnect here, one that my organization tries to correct by getting donations of food that would otherwise end up in landfills from grocery stores, restaurants, and catering companies and redistributing it to people who need it. Yet the situation begs a question that resonates on a personal level as well as a political and structural one: If we have enough to spare, then why aren't we sparing it?

This is a systemic problem that government, entire industries, and large corporations play a part in. But so do individuals. So do we, which is why I invite you to examine the role you play. How much do you throw away from your fridge or pantry each month? How much do you let spoil or neglect to use before the expiration date? If you're like most people, you're probably not even sure. To get a better idea, try this simple experiment: Get a large plastic bin with a lid to keep on your porch, fire escape, or in your backyard for the next month. Then, every time you intend to throw away those leftovers or wilting vegetables, toss them in the bin instead. Go through your cupboards and pantry and put into the bin anything that's expired. Then, at the end of the month, look at how much you've wasted. If you're anything like the average American, you waste about a pound of food per day.[5]

As you're looking at how full your bin has become, ask yourself some of those mindful questions I've been talking about. Ask things like: Why do so many people feel comfortable throwing so much away, but uncomfortable giving their pocket change to someone who's asking for it? We're talking about an amount of money you could probably lose in your couch cushions or clothes dryer without even noticing, but then suddenly feel like holding onto tightly when you see someone begging on the street. Does that make a lot of sense to you?

Other questions to ask yourself: How does it feel when I waste what I have? How does it feel when I walk past people begging on the street without acknowledging them or their needs?

When we do these things, we're not just denying other people the gifts we could be giving them, we're also denying ourselves the opportunity to give. We deny ourselves the pleasure, the connection, the sense of purpose and empowerment that come from being a giver. Remember in the last chapter when I talked about how feelings of disconnection, depression, and anxiety are all on the rise? Well, ask yourself which attitude is more likely to contribute to these kinds of feelings: an attitude of scarcity or an attitude of abundance? And on the flipside, which is more likely to contribute to your happiness?

❤ HEARTWORK ❤

1) Think about how much you willingly give to others on a regular basis, particularly people who are not members of your immediate circle of friends and family.

2) Next, think about how much you waste on a regular basis: How much food do you end up throwing away? How many things do you buy that you end up not using much or even at all?

3) Now imagine gathering up everything you've thought of in each of these two categories and putting them on opposite sides of an enormous scale. If you did that, would the scales be balanced? Or would they tip in one direction or the other? Which direction?

4) Ask yourself what you would like to see happen: Would you prefer to see yourself as a more *giving* person or a more *wasteful* one?

OUR VIEWS ABOUT "THE OTHER"

Human beings really seem to enjoy judging each other. The way social media is often (maybe even *most often*) used is a prime example. And it doesn't seem to matter much whether we know the person we're judging. This is another area where more mindfulness could really benefit us: being mindful of the way we think about others and often judge, dismiss, or dehumanize them without realizing it. When I talked before about not giving your pocket change to someone even though you've probably lost that much in the laundry, some version of the following thought may have gone through your mind: "It's my hard-earned money to lose. Why should I give it to someone who doesn't deserve it?"

Most, if not all of us, like to think of ourselves as good people, but at the same time it's pretty common among us humans to have instinctive negative reactions to what we perceive as weakness—whether that means someone who is sick, elderly, disabled, mentally ill, poor, or living on the street. Sometimes even someone we care about who's asking us for help or a favor can draw out our annoyance and negativity.

Research suggests that this kind of reaction may be hardwired into our DNA, a primitive, "survival of the fittest" instinct to see the weak as prey.[6] It may be a common, even natural reaction, but once again we need to ask ourselves if it makes a lot of sense and if it's beneficial to us and to the world around us. After all, we don't live in a primitive world anymore, and our ability to literally hunt or be hunted is no longer what makes us successful human beings. The good news is that we can change our reactions when we bring awareness to them, even the ones that are hardwired. We can replace old stories with new, more accurate, more empowering, and more loving ones if more truthful, more empowered, and more loving is the kind of people we want to be.

I hear the same kind of "stories"—or, if we're being honest, excuses—all the time when I speak to people about the work I do. "I would give more, but . . . "

"But, what?" I often ask. "What's stopping you?"

Some of the most common reasons I get reveal that many of us have pretty poor attitudes toward other people. "Giving people handouts just teaches them to be dependent" is a common perception, but I've never seen any research to back it up. In fact, if you think about it in terms of children and how they're raised, it seems to me that the exact opposite is true. Children are constantly being given handouts unless they're being neglected. They have to be given everything in the beginning because they don't have the ability to provide for themselves. But that doesn't mean that all children grow up to be freeloaders. In fact, it's by receiving the right things in the right way that children grow up knowing how to care for themselves and having enough self-esteem to do it.

We may not like to think of ourselves this way, but haven't we all been given handouts at one time or another, even as adults? Has no one ever helped you get a job or get a deal on something you wanted? Has no one ever given you a loan or outright paid for something you needed or wanted? When those things happened, did it make you more dependent or did it help you become independent and capable of providing for yourself?

I also get: "People will just waste what I give them. They'll spend it on drugs or alcohol or something else that's unnecessary at best, destructive at worst." And yet, as I just mentioned, there's so much waste happening already. Are some kinds of waste better than others? Maybe so. I don't want to enable anyone's destructive habits either, but we have to wonder what we're sacrificing by prioritizing this thought above all others. For example, while drug abuse among the homeless population is difficult to determine, the National Institutes of Health has estimated that only ten to fifteen percent of people living on the streets abuse drugs.[7] People who use this as a reason not to give are often surprised by how low the percentage is. I don't lie to them. It's possible that something you give someone will be wasted or used in a way you wouldn't want, but most of the time it won't. In which case, you have to ask yourself: Are you willing to sacrifice all the people who could really make good use of your gifts in order to avoid the minority of people who won't?

What's more, who's to say that a drug addict isn't worthy of your time or a plate of food? If you or someone you love has struggled with addiction, then you might hope that not everyone feels that way. After all, how can we expect people to become capable of turning their lives around if they are cut off from others and deprived of basic necessities? We never know what might make the difference to someone. It might even be our gift that inspires change.

Often these kinds of knee-jerk reactions, these "I would give, but . . . " stories, are ways of protecting ourselves, of avoiding unpleasant or painful realities, or of simply reacting without thinking. After all, if we take time to consider, we might realize that it's not so hard to understand how someone might end up with an addiction. Life can be a struggle even when we do have a roof over our heads and a reliable income. Imagine what it would be like if we didn't. Is it so hard to understand that some people who are living in tough circumstances might reach for something to help them cope? Is it so impossible to empathize with someone for doing so? After all, you might be tempted to do the same if you found yourself in the same position.

I have similar responses for those who express this concern: "People won't appreciate my effort, or worse, they'll take advantage of me." Nothing in life is one hundred percent risk free, and giving is no different. When we take a new job, move to a new place, make a new friend, or start a romantic relationship, there's always the possibility that we'll be hurt in some way. When we give, sometimes our gifts will be rejected, and rejection hurts. Sometimes people will ask us to give more than we should, and that's not fair. But if we prepare ourselves, if we're mindful about what we're doing, and if we give with intention, then the good experiences will always far outweigh the bad.

What we need to do is stop pretending we know what will happen when we open ourselves up to giving. So many of us have a tendency to assume the worst in people. There are always reasons behind this, and sometimes they're even understandable ones. We've all been hurt by someone, and we tend to carry those wounds with us into our interactions with others. But we have to ask ourselves if those wounds we carry are going to be healed by cutting ourselves off from others, by shutting down our hearts, by denying our basic giving instincts, and by *not* trying to make things better.

It can be hard. Giving can feel like a vulnerable act if we don't trust people. It helps to remember that there are people out there praying for the gifts we can give right now. Instead of focusing on what could go wrong, think about what it could mean to them—and to you—to be the answer to those prayers. We deny ourselves opportunities for meaning and joy in our lives when we assume, often without real evidence, that giving isn't worth it, or that the people we could be giving to aren't worth it. Imagine if someone, without even knowing you, decided the same about you?

ACKNOWLEDGE YOUR FEELINGS—AND SPEAK TO THEM

The stories we tell ourselves don't come out of nowhere. They come from real experiences. When we're young, we're told stories by others, which help us learn about and make sense of the world. As we grow older, we may continue to accept those stories and act on them without examining them. In this way, we often let life just happen to us rather than admitting that there's always room for resetting and expanding our way of thinking beyond our past experiences.

As we get older, we begin to make up stories of our own about our experiences, often in reaction to how they make us feel. For example, someone might hurt us by rejecting us when we reach out to them, and that experience makes us fearful of being hurt again. So we tell ourselves the story that it's better to keep to ourselves instead of putting ourselves out there with new people. Why risk getting hurt when we don't have to?

Another story many of us tell ourselves comes from the anger that wells up in us about this world and the f❤cked-up way it works. It is painful and it is infuriating to look around and see how the power structures in our society not only allow suffering, but often encourage it. The story most often told as a result is that the problems we face are just too big and too ingrained. We can't possibly do anything about them, so why try when it's obvious that we'll fail?

It does us no good to pretend that the world isn't messed up in certain ways. The questions for all of us are: If that's the reality, are we content to just ignore it? Are we okay with simply throwing up our hands and saying, "There's nothing I can do about it anyway!" Is that the kind of people we want to be? And are we sure there's nothing we can do? What makes us so certain? Have we even tried?

I said it before, but I'm going to say it again because it's a point I see people missing far too often: There's always room for expanding our way of thinking beyond our past experiences. There's always room for growth. There's always room for better and more empowering choices.

Deep down I think we all know there's more we can do. Not to save the world—as I said before, that's not a job that any one person needs to take on—but to save our own hearts and to save our own souls. When we're young, before we experience the hurt that comes from other people's callousness or cruelty, before we come to understand how indifferent our society can be, giving love and care to the people around us is a pure and innate expression of our soul. We once smiled at people freely, made little things to give to them, shared what we had. We didn't worry about being rejected or not having enough. We just did it as an expression of our soul.

It makes me think about all the adults I've met who say they aren't creative or that they don't have much of an imagination. When I hear that, I always wonder how that could possibly be. Have you ever met a five-year-old who said she wasn't creative? Who wasn't thrilled to get his hands dirty with finger paints or break into a new box of crayons? We're all born with the capacity to imagine and create, just like we are born with the capacity to be giving and loving.

Yet somewhere along the way, some of us unlearned these abilities or forgot that we have them. When we're mindful of that fact, when we acknowledge that we still have the capacity to imagine, create, and give, then what we do with it becomes a choice.

We have to start by accepting where we are and what we're feeling because that's the only way we can be accountable to ourselves. This can be uncomfortable, but being mindful means looking where it hurts instead of turning away. We all have hurt, fear, anger, and more to deal with in our lives, but the question is, do we stop there and live in those feelings, or do we want something more? It reminds me of a friend whose boyfriend was cheating on her. I knew it. Everyone knew it. She knew it too, but she wasn't ready to accept it, which meant she stayed in the relationship and remained unhappy for a really long time. We can't start to make changes until we first accept the reality of our situation. That's always going to be true no matter what aspect of life we're talking about.

If we want something more out of our lives, then we have to hold ourselves accountable for doing the work. This is really about changing our hearts, because when someone's heart feels differently, they act differently.

The alternative is being stuck in your hurt and anger. It's cutting yourself off from others and dwelling in your unhappiness. It's telling yourself stories about why you can't connect with people and making excuses for why you don't have more to give. I'm not saying it's easy to do the work, but I do think it's easy to decide which choice is going to make for a better life.

❤ HEARTWORK ❤

Ask yourself: *What stories do I tell myself? What reasons do I give, to myself or others, for not being more caring and helpful toward people in my community?*

Write the reasons down in a list—as many of them as you can think of. Then read the list aloud to yourself and take some time to consider each one.

Now, one by one, speak to each of your stories. Could there be another way of looking at things? Could you reset your thinking in some way? Imagine that these aren't your stories, but someone else's, and it's your job to simply take another point of view. What might that be? For every reason you've given why you *can't* give more to the people around you, try flipping it on its head and write down reasons why you *can* and why you might want to.

YOUR PRIVILEGE IS SHOWING—SO LET IT SHINE

If you've bought this book for your own interest, growth, or entertainment, then there are some things about you that I can probably guess even though we've never met. Chances are good that you've had at least a basic education. When you were growing up, it's almost certain that at least one person (and probably more than one) gave a damn about you. You almost surely have reliable access to food and shelter, maybe not at every moment in your past, but at least in your present circumstances. We often forget just how much we have in this life and how much we've been given.

"But my life is the way it is because I earned it," you might say. It's not my intention to diminish anyone's talent or hard work, but at the same time I think we all need to remember that we weren't born earning our keep. At least one someone, and probably many someones, have propped us up along the way. We have been given food and shelter. We have been granted an education, at least through high school—and maybe we contributed to our own higher education, or maybe we didn't. We have all been given love and encouragement as we developed our ability to earn what we have. The things I'm talking about are the basic building blocks of a successful life, and yet not everyone is lucky enough to have them.

During the filming of the documentary I made about life on Skid Row, I had a number of encounters that showed me just how different, and privileged, my "real" life was compared to how I'd been living during my time in a tent on the street. One day about a week or so in, I was excited about all the wonderful images the documentary filmmaker had captured, so I decided to go to a nearby frame shop to look at some ways we could display what we'd created.

It was the kind of thing most of us would do without a second thought, but the moment I walked into the store I could feel the energy wasn't right. I'd been wearing the same outfit since shooting began, which had grown gradually dingier and dingier by the day, and I hadn't showered in a week. I'd gotten used to it by that point, so I wasn't even thinking about my appearance as I pushed open the door to the store. I wasn't, but the shopkeeper was. Before I got a chance to do or say anything, my appearance caused a chain reaction.

First, the shopkeeper looked me up and down. Then her face screwed up in obvious disapproval. She didn't even have to think it over; her response was automatic. She walked right over to me before I could get too far away from the door. "What are you doing here," she said with disdain. It wasn't a question. I could tell because, before I could answer, she followed up with a succinct and definite: "Get. Out."

People talk a lot about privilege these days. When they do, they're usually referring to the money people have to spend on things they want and need, or the experiences that money has afforded them. Or they talk about privileges afforded to certain groups of people because of their race, gender, religion, or sexual orientation. They don't usually think about privilege as being something as basic as everyday acceptance in the world around them.

It's a kind of privilege many of us hardly have to consider. When was the last time you walked into a public place only to be told you weren't good enough to be there? Has it ever happened to you? If it has—maybe because of your race or sexual orientation or because you look a little different—I feel you. It's happened to me too. But imagine if it happened not just when you were outside your neighborhood or in an area where people were different from you, but everywhere you went. There are some people in this world who have a hard time finding acceptance anywhere they go.

When I was kicked out of that store, I was furious, but I also realized I was lucky enough to feel angry about it. That's because while I've experienced prejudice in my life, I've also had the privilege of being able to walk into most places and be accepted for no other reason than because I looked the part. I was clean enough, well-dressed enough, attractive enough, confident enough to be let in. And that alone has been an enormous advantage.

When I walked into that frame store, I was the same person I've always been, but on this particular day, based on one quick look, a stranger decided to reject me outright. My heart sank when she did that because I know there are people out there who experience that kind of thing every day. I thought about all the people I've met on Skid Row over the years who have been so kind and welcoming toward me, whose light has shone so bright even in very difficult circumstances. They experience rejection and disgust on a regular basis for no other reason than because they don't have reliable access to a shower or clean clothes. That's it. That's all it takes. Reliable access to a shower and clean clothes is all that separates you, who are worthy of being let in at least somewhere, from someone who gets chased away.

And that's what happened to me after a little more than a week on Skid Row. Imagine what it would be like after years of that kind of treatment. And that was just one of the advantages I couldn't help but notice. Another was that while sleeping on Skid Row, there was a part of my spirit that could never rest. One night my tent got blown over by the wind. Another night, the police went by at four a.m. with their sirens blaring. Even when things were (relatively) quiet, the knowledge that something *could* happen at any moment was inescapable. All that separated me from the harsh world out there was a thin nylon sheet. There's no real sense of safety in that. As a result, I had no way to access the peace I'm used to finding when I need it. That's not to say that my life is stress-free or easy on a typical day, and I'm sure you would say the same about yours, but I've come to rely on the fact that when I need to decompress or ground myself, I can almost always find space in the world for solace if I try. Not everyone is so lucky.

This isn't to say that you should forget about the challenges you face or ignore your own stresses just because someone else might suffer more. This isn't to diminish the work you do every day to make your life function, which is no small feat. This is just a reminder that the hardships we face are only one part of our stories. The word "privilege" can have so many negative connotations, so let's call it something else. Let's call it our gifts. We've all been given so many gifts in this life, beginning with our life itself. We didn't earn that. It was given to us, and I believe it's our responsibility to remember that gift, and all the others we've been given, even as we struggle through the very real challenges in our lives.

If we can do that, then maybe we can find space in our hearts to share those gifts with those who have not been so lucky. You can't share what you don't know you have, which is where greater mindfulness can be so useful. Remember your gifts. Make a conscious effort to pay attention to them in your daily life—at least as much attention as you pay to the things you struggle with. The more you do, the more you'll realize just how much you have to give to this world.

As I said in the beginning of this chapter, the real purpose of becoming more mindful of the way we think is so that we can start to shift our perspective to a view that's not only more loving, but also truer. What I really want people to start saying to themselves is this: "Though I sometimes forget to acknowledge it, it's true that I've been given something good in this life—whether it's my time, my talent, my resources, or my ability to care and to love—so why am I holding onto it so tightly? Why would I waste it? Why not, instead, try giving it to everyone I can? What would it be like to do that?"

This can be a pretty momentous shift for some, so we'll start small. We'll start with simple, intentional actions that I call micro-gestures.

Think about the top five things you want to be more mindful of after reading this chapter. Your list might include unique gifts that you want to share, a story you often tell yourself that you want to think about in a new way, or even a specific person who you feel you haven't given the benefit of the doubt in the past. Write the five things down on a sticky note and put the note on your mirror, on your computer screen, or on the first page of your journal, someplace where you'll look at it every day and be prompted to be more mindful.

3

MICRO-GESTURES WILL CHANGE THE WORLD

How does a lamp burn? Through the continuous input of small drops of oil.
What are these drops of oil in our lamps? They are the small things of daily
life: faithfulness, small words of kindness, a thought for others, our way of
being silent, of looking, of speaking, and of acting."

MOTHER TERESA, *No Greater Love*[1]

People ask me all the time what they can do to make a difference in their community. A question I get almost as frequently is whether I feel like the work I do is worth it. Do I believe it really makes a difference? Of course I do or I wouldn't do it, but I get why people ask. Scan the headlines on any given day and it can easily feel like the world's problems are intractable and overwhelming. But I never get overwhelmed. Truly, never. That's because I've come to understand something important that keeps me motivated to continue my work: Changing the world is not my responsibility. And it's not yours either. Like my grandmother said, all I need to do is to take responsibility for doing my part. That's all any of us needs to do. If enough of us do that, then together we can make this world a better place.

My advice everywhere I go, every time I'm asked how one person can make a difference, is always the same: instead of being overwhelmed by the magnitude of the world's problems, focus on your side of the street and do something, anything, to impact just one of those problems. I call it the micro-gesture, and there are opportunities for micro-gestures all around us, all the time. Unfortunately, they're opportunities that many of us are missing.

WHY START WITH A MICRO-GESTURE?

If there is only one idea you take from this book, I hope it will be this: every single one of us can make a positive difference. We don't need to gain any special skills or change anything about how our lives work. We don't need any more power or money or time than we already have. We don't need to be any different than how we are right now. We just have to remember that even one small stone can make big ripples in the water if thrown with enough force. Each one of us can be that small stone.

A lot of times we go through life just worrying about how we're going to make things work. We're focused on our own problems, and we forget that we impact other people all the time—every time we interact, or choose not to interact, with someone we come into contact with. If we can be mindful of that idea and keep it in the back of our minds throughout the day, then we can move on to the second Be: Be intentional. We can intentionally make small shifts that allow our interactions to be more meaningful. With the right mindset and intention, we can have a more positive impact on people, and it doesn't even need to be that hard.

Always remember: even small gestures can have big impacts. When you see someone who looks like she's having a bad day, you can give her a smile or a kind word. When you see someone being mistreated or bullied, you can step in and redirect the conversation. When you see someone being ignored, you can acknowledge him and help him feel seen. When you see someone who could use a little help, you can offer your hand.

These are micro-gestures: simple, easy things that anyone can do. All you need is to be mindful of the people around you and set an intention to make a positive impact when and where you can. In many cases, you'll see the difference you've made immediately. You'll be able to tell by the look on someone's face or the words of thanks they offer in return. But even when that doesn't happen, it's important to keep in mind that the effort is worth it. It's worth it for other people's sake and it's worth it for your own. You will always be able to look yourself in the mirror and say, "At least I tried." Besides, we don't always know in the moment the impact we're having on people when we choose to give a f♥ck about them.

Not long ago, I was speaking at an event hosted by author and former 2020 presidential candidate Marianne Williamson in Beverly Hills, a place that's miles away both geographically and metaphorically from Skid Row. So I was taken aback when a young, good-looking guy, who appeared to be on the verge of tears, came up to me afterward. Without saying a word, he wrapped his arms around me and gave me a forceful hug.

The man looked vaguely familiar, but I didn't really recognize him until he stammered out: "I just had to thank you. You gave me coconut water seven months ago when I was high and had collapsed on the street."

I understood what was happening then. It was the kind of thing I do for people all the time without thinking much about it. I tried to tell the man that he didn't have to thank me—that I was glad to help—but he had more to say, something that he really wanted me to understand.

"Most people just walked by me that day or stepped over me without even acknowledging what was happening," he continued. "And I didn't want to ask anyone for help. I was too embarrassed, and I didn't want to be judged. By that point in my life, a lot of my friends and family knew about my drug problem, and I always felt judged by them. But you didn't judge me at all, and I didn't need to ask for your help. You just walked right up to me with a smile and said, 'Love, you're dehydrated—you need something to drink.' And you gave me that drink. You stood with me while I drank it, and then you told me to take care of myself, got in your car, and left."

That was it. It was a micro-gesture, just one moment that I'd had with this man, which he remembered much more clearly than I did. But it had made a difference. His name was Paul, and Paul told me that he decided right then and there that if a stranger could care that much about him, then maybe it was time he tried caring at least that much about himself. After I left, he picked himself up and went to rehab to check himself in. By the time I saw him in Beverly Hills, he'd gotten off drugs, off the street, and back together with his fiancée. He had turned his life totally around.

It was a turning point for him, and for me too. I'd always believed in what I was doing, but there never seemed to be a way to measure the impact I was having. There never seemed to be a way to show that I was making a real and lasting difference. But all of a sudden, here was proof standing right in front of me. It had been such a small gesture on my part. It never occurred to me, even after all my years of doing this, that an act so small could change someone's life. But it had.

It's for that reason and so many others that I tell people to just *try* helping someone out, with no expectations, for no reason other than because you see a need and you know you can fulfill it. It doesn't have to be some big thing,

MICRO-GESTURE: A DEFINITION

Noun. A small, simple, intentional act of love or caring for another person that can be done by anyone, anywhere, at any time.

just a micro-gesture. Do this once, with the right intention, and I guarantee you'll *feel* the difference. Make it a way of life, and you'll *become* different. And just maybe, someone else will become different too.

THE MICRO-GESTURE IN FIVE SIMPLE STEPS

The most important thing about a micro-gesture is that anyone can do it. It doesn't have to be about helping people who are hungry, displaced, or living on the streets, like I do. It can be about helping anyone who could use it. What's more, it doesn't have to be difficult. It doesn't have to take a lot of time. There's really no excuse *not* to try it.

Let's start with the basic steps, and then I'll spend some time expanding on each one:

1) Open your eyes and look around.

We need to start by taking our blinders off and getting into the habit of paying attention to what's happening around us. In other words, we need to start by being mindful. Try to let go of your preconceived notions about people or situations and just notice: Who around you might be hurting? Who could use some help? Who has a need that you could fulfill?

2) When you notice someone, take intentional action.

Do something to connect. This could be something simple, or it could be something more involved. For example: instead of staring silently ahead in an elevator, as most people do when they're awkwardly packed together, pick out someone who looks like she could use a lift and pay her a compliment. When you see someone hanging out in front of your local gas station, grocery store, Walmart, or drive-through, don't just walk past the person. Instead, go over and say: "I see you every time I come here, and I would love to know your name so next time I can say hello."

3) Without expectation, notice the effect.

Take some time to consider the impact that a simple act of seeing someone and connecting, even briefly, has on that person. And also on you. Your smile will typically be met with a smile. A genuine compliment will almost always elicit a thank you. We have to remember that it's a universal feeling to want to be seen, acknowledged, and appreciated for who we are. When we can do that for someone, it's empowering for us as well.

4) Next time, step it up a little in generosity.

The next time you see that person in front of the grocery store, say hello and ask if he needs anything. Say something like: "I'm going inside to do my shopping, and I'm wondering if you've eaten today. Can I bring you back some lunch?" (You'll find a whole range of additional suggestions in the menu of micro-gestures at the back of the book.)

5) Make micro-gestures a regular practice.

String a few micro-gestures together over the course of several days or a week. Do this for a few weeks in a row, and it will start to become second nature. That's what we want: for micro-gestures to become part of your regular routine.

TAKING NOTICE

In the last chapter we talked about being mindful of your own ways of thinking and your own behaviors. Now I'm asking you to turn that same mindful gaze onto others—onto what they're thinking, what they're feeling, and what they're experiencing in their lives. For many of us, this will require a slight redistribution of our time, energy, and focus. It will mean making an effort to put down the newspaper and get off social media from time to time. It will mean making an occasional effort to stop focusing so intently on Twitter wars, celebrity gossip, political battles in Washington, DC, and depressing headlines from the other side of the world.

I'm not asking anyone to become completely disconnected or uninformed. I'm not asking anyone to ditch social media either. I use it all the time to connect with volunteers and donors, to spread the word about the work my organization does, and to give a voice and a face to the people we serve. It's an invaluable tool for these purposes, but we all know that it has its downsides too. What I'm asking for is balance, because let's face it, none of us are going to change ourselves or make things better in the world if we never get out from behind our screens. I'm suggesting that you focus at least as much of your attention and energy on connecting with the people who exist in real time, all around you, as you spend focused on the world "out there." Take more time to notice the people you can actually reach out and touch—and become better informed about what's happening in your own backyard.

In the first chapter of this book, I talked about the epidemic of loneliness and disconnection that our culture is facing. I'm convinced that a significant contributor to this is the fact that so many of us spend so much time connecting with people over social media rather than seeing and experiencing them firsthand. In the same way, we spend a lot of time focused on problems that we don't have the power or capacity to fix. Maybe you don't like who is president, or you're infuriated about the country's immigration policy. Maybe you're truly saddened by the tragedy that happened on the other side of the world. I'm not saying you shouldn't care about these things, but what can you *do* about them right now, in this moment? By all means vote in the next election and support candidates who represent your values. Send money to help in an emergency if you can. But in the meantime, ask yourself if being frustrated and sad, or worse, voicing your frustration into the Twitter void, really makes a difference. Does it do anything to change the situation? Does it do anything to make you feel better?

In many ways, what we choose to focus on is what defines us. If we choose to focus all or most of our attention on our anger or dismay about situations we cannot affect on a day-to-day basis, I'm not sure how that's going to make us feel anything but angrier, sadder, and more disempowered. On the flipside, human beings are hardwired to connect with one another. We're social creatures by nature. By that I mean we need tangible, reach-out-and-touch-each-other type of connections. My hope is that we can start to see each one of those connections, whether it's with a stranger or someone we know, as an opportunity to empower ourselves and others by bringing more positivity into the world and sharing our gifts.

♥ HEARTWORK ♥

Ask yourself: *How much of my time and energy do I spend worrying or getting upset about problems and concerns that I can't really fix, or even impact? How much of my time and energy do I spend on making a difference where I can—in my own neighborhood or community?*

Take some time to consider these questions, and then, after you've answered them both, compare the results. Do you spend more of your time and energy on worrying and getting upset, or on trying to make things better? If it's the first, consider whether it might feel better to distribute your resources differently.

Think back over the past week and make a list of all the moments, no matter how small, to which you could have brought a little more love and caring. Was there someone who could have used a hug? Was there a friend who could have benefited from a check-in call or text? Was there a moment when you could have put down your phone and paid closer attention to your child or partner? Did you pass anyone on the street asking for help? Name every opportunity that came your way so that you can start training your brain to take notice.

TAKING INTENTIONAL ACTION

In the previous chapter we looked closely at mindfulness as one of the three main components for Loving Without Reason. The second is about intention. We've spent some time being mindful of ourselves and others. Now we'll make an effort to be intentional about our actions toward other people.

If you really think about it, you'll probably find that you aren't all that intentional about many of your actions during a typical day. Most of what we do comes from habit or instinct, not intention. When we walk past someone on the street who is asking for change or suffering like Paul was, it's not usually because we've intentionally chosen to be callous and uncaring. It's an instinctive reaction, a way of protecting ourselves from confronting a situation that is likely to bring up negative feelings. Or, if we live in an urban area where we encounter moments like these on a regular basis, it may just be our habit to ignore it so that we can get on with our day.

Similarly, when a spouse or a friend acts rudely toward us, it's often our instinct to lash back. We don't think about it; we just do it. It's the same when someone raises his or her voice to us. When you're in a disagreement with someone, yelling tends to lead to more yelling. We've all seen this happen. In fact, we've probably all taken part in this kind of yelling match, which gets louder and louder as one party matches the volume of the other, but goes nowhere in the end. These kinds of reactive and habitual ways of treating people deserve our mindful focus so that we can become more intentional about how we respond. The question we need to ask ourselves here is this: Are these ways of treating people really making things any better, for them or for us?

Another important thing to consider here is that we can be intentional not just about how we act and respond, but about who we choose to help. I believe in giving people the benefit of the doubt. Just because someone has a problem with drugs or has done something wrong in the past doesn't mean that they're unworthy of a plate of food or a moment of my time. However, we've all met people who try to take advantage of our caring or wear us out with continual requests for help. Becoming a doormat is not what Love Without Reason is about. This is really important because all too often I hear people talk about how they're just tired and depleted. Often they feel that way because they think they're being giving when what they're really doing is giving themselves away.

I mentor a young woman who is an up-and-coming videographer. She's so very talented, but she's also new to the city and still finding her feet in her career. It's not an easy field to break into, so she started a collective of four aspiring videographers of similar age and experience to herself. The idea was that they could share knowledge and equipment, partner to get work, and support one another as they build their careers.

It was a great idea. The problem was that the group wasn't working the way she'd envisioned it, but she didn't want to admit it. She was putting a lot of effort into helping the others by getting them jobs and giving them feedback on their work but was getting very little in return. One guy in the group even actively put her down on a regular basis, making her feel like she wasn't as talented as she clearly is.

This isn't what I mean by GAF. Giving shouldn't make you feel like you're being taken advantage of or mistreated. Fulfilling someone else's need is not supposed to create a need in you. For example, I've said before that if you waste a lot of food or have extras cluttering up your cupboards, then giving some of that away is a great way to share your gifts. But if you're struggling to feed your family, I would never want you to give away so much that you find yourself turning to your local food pantry at the end of month, or worse, going without.

Giving takes practice like anything else. And like any other practice, the more you do it, the better you'll get at it. So don't beat yourself up when you make mistakes along the way and someone does take your gifts for granted. It's all part of the journey. What you can do, however, is pay attention to the warning signs that mistakes are being made. If it doesn't feel good to give to someone, be mindful of that. Stop and ask yourself why. Maybe it's because you gave with attachment—meaning you unfairly expected something in return. Or maybe it's because you gave to the wrong person, to someone who was looking to drain you rather than be present and appreciative of your gifts.

There's a simple (if not always easy) solution when you give to the wrong person: stop giving to that person and save your gifts for those who will appreciate them. When the woman I mentor realized the dynamic in her group wasn't working for her, she decided to disband it and stand on her own. She and her career are better for it, but I told her not to regret the effort she'd put into it. She learned a valuable lesson about how giving our gifts does not mean giving away our power.

In fact, for many of us it's probably a good idea to start off by focusing our micro-gestures on strangers and acquaintances rather than family and close friends. You'll have to decide for yourself what works best for you, but the truth is, the closer the relationship, the more baggage it tends to carry. Practicing your giving in situations that are less fraught can be really valuable. It can help you learn to be more intentional and see more clearly the purpose and benefits that giving can bring into your life. It can also teach you some lessons that can be used to inform all your relationships going forward. In a later chapter, we'll talk about bringing more love to those closest to you and what to do when love becomes labor, as can often happen with the relationships we rely on the most.

GIVING CREATES MEANING

What I find time and time again is that, when done mindfully and with intention, helping people and having a positive impact creates a kind of high. It just feels good to make someone smile. It feels purposeful to do something that fulfills a need or helps someone feel valued. It's that high that keeps me going. And it gets easier as you go. You begin by setting an intention to brighten someone's day or help someone out, but pretty soon it will become second nature. You'll see opportunities all around you, and you'll feel more equipped and empowered to make good use of them.

Not long ago, a friend decided to try doing what she'd seen me do numerous times when we were out together: walk up to a stranger in need and offer help. She had stopped by a drugstore one afternoon to pick up some dental floss. It was the most boring of chores, but it became something more when she noticed a man outside rubbing his toes.

"You look like you could use some warm socks," she said to him.

He looked up at her, unsure at first, but when he saw her smiling, he smiled back. "Yeah, it's been cold out here in the mornings. Wet too, and these don't help much," he said, pointing to his plastic flip-flops.

"You know, I'm going into the drugstore to pick up a few things. I bet they have socks. Do you want me to get you some?"

"Yes, that would be great," he said. He looked so pleased that she wanted to do more. She asked him if he wanted anything else.

"Maybe some food if you can," he said tentatively.

"Okay, what do you like?"

He mentioned some pouches of tuna that he knew the store carried, which were easy to open and tasted good. He was reluctant to ask for anything more even though she offered again, so she decided that she would put together a bag of things that would last him a few days.

The man's name was Jason, which my friend still remembered a month later when she told me the story. "The thing about it that was so interesting," she said to me, "was that I was having a completely dull day. I was on my way to the dentist. I had arrived early, so I decided to pick up some dental floss because I knew we needed some. It was completely forgettable stuff, and yet I remember it all now because of Jason.

"There are times in our lives when we just need to get things done, and then there are times in our lives that are more meaningful by nature. It never occurred to me before to try to combine them, to try to make a simple trip to the drugstore a more meaningful experience. But on that day, it was. Now I wonder if I couldn't be bringing more meaning into my life on a regular basis. If I can make it happen while shopping for dental floss, there have to be more chances out there for life to feel even fuller."

I completely agreed. This is why, when doing your micro-gestures, step number three is important not to skip: "Without expectation, notice the effect." Take a moment to notice what has happened after you do something for someone else. Your gesture will have an effect, on you and on the other person, and it's those effects that infuse the moment with meaning.

WHY I GIVE A F♥CK . . .

"I care about my own life so I care about other people's. And I have loved ones, family members—I think about them and what could happen to them. I see myself and I see my loved ones in the people I try to help, even if I don't know them."

VENUS
nonprofit president, age 34

EXPAND YOUR GENEROSITY

When I talk about giving more, a lot of people worry that they don't have enough time or money to spare. They worry that if they're too generous, then they'll be taking things away from themselves and their family. But giving shouldn't make you feel deprived. In fact, it should make you feel just the opposite.

This brings us to the third of the three Be's: Be generous. I think too many people have a narrow definition of what it means to give generously. They think they need to sit down and write big checks at the end of the month if they want to feel like they're really making a difference. And sure, that's a great thing to do if you won't miss the money. But if you will, if you're worried that you should be contributing to your kid's college fund instead of to a nonprofit, then put your money in the college fund. And give something else.

Even if you do make big donations or go to work at a service job every day, I would still challenge you to find new ways to expand your generosity. While those things are totally valid and necessary things to do in our society, they don't always exercise the giving muscle in the intentional way I'm describing because they often aren't a direct experience. I'm really talking about engaging with the community around you, noticing what needs people might have, and then extending yourself in whatever ways you can to meet some of that need, often with no intermediaries, no organization in between. Just you seeing a need and you fulfilling it.

This is something we can all do, no matter what our profession or circumstances, no matter what sort of person we are, and we can do it by learning to think more creatively about giving. Start by asking yourself some basic questions, like: What do I have a lot of in my life? What am I good at? What particular knowledge or skills do I have that not everyone else has?

As you answer these questions, don't just think about the answers as your own attributes. Think about them as things you have to share. These are your gifts, and I want you to start thinking about how you can use them to help others.

Once you've made a list of your gifts, consider who might be able to benefit from them besides you and your family. Do you have a talent like teaching yoga? Offer a free class at your local homeless shelter or community center. Know how to write killer resumes? Offer that skill for free to someone who is looking for a job. Are you a great listener? Work with foster kids or mentor a child in your area. Do you love to read? How about reading to people who have lost their vision or to seniors who would like the company. Do you have a green thumb? Bring some of your homegrown flowers or potted plants to your local hospital or nursing home. Are you great with animals? Offer to help care for an elderly person's pet or walk the dog of a sick or injured person in your neighborhood.

I could go on and on. The possibilities for turning your gifts into micro-gestures are as endless as your imagination. You can give your goods, your time, your talents, or your money. You can give your love, your respect, and your attention. The real secret behind it all is this: It doesn't really matter what you give. It just matters that you make a point of giving. Everyone has something to offer. Literally everyone. There are no exceptions.

Even on Skid Row, a place where people have so little to spare, I see people giving to one another all the time. My friend Ms. Brenda ended up on Skid Row when she was in her late forties. She had lived in a foster home growing up, but it was more of a place where she worked for her keep than a home where she was cared for. Her foster "mother" made her cook and clean in exchange for her room and board. When she turned eighteen and the State of California was no longer required to look after her, her former foster mom offered her a deal: she would continue to provide Ms. Brenda with a place to live in exchange for her taking care of the house and the woman's grandkids. She was essentially the unpaid, live-in help.

Ms. Brenda stuck to that bargain for decades. When her former foster mom got older, she took care of her as well. But then the woman passed away, and her children, who had rarely been around to help care for their own mom, kicked Ms. Brenda out of the only home she'd ever known. They wanted to sell it, and they didn't care what happened to Ms. Brenda. Having nowhere else to go, she ended up on Skid Row, and she has rarely left the area since.

That was more than a dozen years ago. Ms. Brenda is in her early sixties now and she still wants to feel useful, just like we all do. That's why she gets up every morning and cleans her side of the street. She says she's been cleaning all her life, and she likes to keep things neat. But she doesn't just clean the area around her own tent. She tidies up around her neighbors' tents as well and then continues on down the block. I don't know about you, but I personally feel a whole lot better when my home is clean and organized. That's a feeling that's hard to come by when you're living on the street, but Ms. Brenda regularly provides it for the people around her. It's her micro-gesture, and she does it every single day. It's what she has to give, and her neighbors love her for it.

♥ HEARTWORK ♥

To help expand your generosity and think more creatively about what you have to give, ask yourself:

What do I have a lot of in my life?

What am I good at?

What knowledge or skills do I have that not everyone else has?

Think broadly about the potential answers to these questions, and be creative. I like to break the possibilities down into four categories:

1) **Goods:** This includes things like food, clothes, kitchen items, toiletries, used computers or vehicles, practically anything you don't need anymore. If it was useful to you at one point and is still in good shape, chances are someone else can make use of it now.

2) **Time:** Don't think of this category only in terms of the minutes or hours you might have to spend on someone, but also as including the attributes you might be able to bring to a person or situation if you took the time—like your kindness, strength, positive outlook, outgoingness, empathy, or so many other things that can be helpful to someone in a difficult situation.

3) **Talents:** You might be great at writing, cooking, graphic design, accounting, childcare, fixing cars, photography, or any number of other things. Whether you do it professionally or as a dedicated hobby, some person or organization out there could surely use your skills and knowledge.

4) **Money:** This one is more obvious, but don't think about it only in terms of large checks written to charitable organizations. If you have an extra $5 for a cup of coffee for someone who is out in the cold on a rainy day, it can really make a difference.

Jot down everything you can think of in each of these categories. Then think about how you might be able to share the things on your list with someone else. Who might need or benefit from them? How might you go about distributing these things to others?

TURNING MICRO-GESTURES INTO A REGULAR PRACTICE

Once you start doing a few micro-gestures, you might find that it's hard to stop. For example, once you start noticing the people asking for change outside your local drive-through or drugstore, you'll find that it's hard to simply walk past them the next time without acknowledging them. Once you start making the effort to take your excess food to a shelter or food drive, it becomes hard not to think about it every time you're inclined to throw something away. GAF on a regular basis changes the way we see things and the way we see people. It changes the way we interact with the world.

Once you start your micro-gestures, you'll also start to notice that it usually feels pretty good to do them. There will be times when you encounter someone who isn't receptive to your gifts, but by and large, giving in this way is a memorable and positive experience for both the giver and the receiver. You may find that it becomes almost addictive as a way to infuse positivity into your daily life.

So once you start to give a f♥ck, just keep giving. Let one micro-gesture turn into two, then ten, and then a hundred. Give to more people more often. Find new ways to offer your gifts. As I said before, be creative and look for opportunities. Step it up in generosity whenever and wherever you can.

One of the best ways to turn your micro-gestures into a regular practice of giving is to prepare yourself for it. Now that you're more mindful, you're likely to see people who could use some help on a regular basis. This is going to be true even when it's not the most convenient time for you to stop and connect. Maybe you're running late for an appointment or you're on your way to work. Maybe you have your kids in the car and they're antsy and impatient to get home. These are times when a little preparation can go a long way. You're more likely to give if you have a plan and some tools ready to make giving a little easier on yourself.

Some suggestions for getting prepared to give include:

> **Keep water and granola bars in your car for when you drive past someone asking for help, like at a highway exit.** These are great things to have on hand especially if you're uncomfortable giving cash.

> **Keep small, giveaway goods in your bag or purse for when you pass someone on the street.** Just make sure it's things that are easy to open and use. No cans of food requiring a can opener, please.

> **Pack your wallet with five-dollar bills.** When you connect with people on a regular basis, you may find that you're more comfortable giving cash to

people you know. I suggest five dollars because one dollar just isn't enough to buy much anymore, not even a cup of coffee in most places.

Fill your wallet with gift cards. This is a great substitute for cash. A lot of people living on the street are really comforted by a fresh, warm cup of coffee, so a gift card to a local coffee shop is a great idea. Or to a grocery store or restaurant so they can buy what they want for themselves. (Just remember to get the cards directly from the stores where they'll be used because there's a lot of fraud that happens with gift cards, especially the ones that are on display at chain drugstores and grocery stores.)

Collect freebees. Every time I stay at a hotel, I gather up the bottles of shampoo, conditioner, and lotion. Whenever I'm at a conference, I take the gift bag even though I don't need any more stuff in my life. A friend gets regular food deliveries from a company that always offers free samples of new products to try. Gather up things like these and put together gift bags (you can use those free totes everyone seems to be giving away these days) to bring to your local shelter, homeless community, or senior center.

Make a regular appointment. Spontaneous giving is great—I'm all for helping wherever and whenever you can—but it's also a good idea to make a plan for giving. After all, if we put things on our calendar, we're more likely to do them, so carve out some regular time on your schedule. You might volunteer at a school or a daycare center once a month. Or you might choose the last weekend of the month to put together your care packages and take them to a shelter. Whatever it is, make an effort to be consistent about it.

A granola bar here, a care package there. These may seem like small things, but I think we often underestimate the power of small acts and the profound difference they can make. And making that difference is so very doable. I was explaining my philosophy of micro-gestures to Tal Rabinowitz, founder of The DEN Meditation centers in Los Angeles, on her podcast once, and even though she was already someone who made a point of giving back, she said the idea inspired her all the more. "Something about calling it 'micro' made it feel 'macro,'" she said later. "It made me ask myself, 'Why aren't I conscious of doing this all the time?'" Once you experience how simple GAF can be, I hope you too will be inspired to do it more and more.

One thing to keep in mind is that it's not just what you give, but how you give it that matters. The energy you bring to your giving is as important as the gift itself—that's a crucial component of this, which we'll talk about in the next chapter.

We must remember that love is in the details, which is why small acts have the power to make big impacts. Just ask Paul, the ex-addict who credited one micro-gesture with changing the course of his life. Micro-gestures have the power to change people. And if you make giving through micro-gestures a regular practice, you'll find the practice has the power to change you as well. So why not let it?

❤ HEARTWORK ❤

Think about a time recently when you had a negative interaction with someone. Maybe it was a falling out you had with a friend. Maybe it was an argument you got into with a stranger at the store. Maybe it was about angry or derisive comments you posted on Facebook or Nextdoor.

Think back to the beginning of the interaction and ask yourself: What was my intention? What did I want to get out of that moment?

Then think about the end of the exchange: What actually resulted from it?

If, for example, your intention with your friend was to let her know that your feelings were hurt by something she said and to feel some relief from that hurt, then how did that go? Did the interaction make you feel better? Or do you now feel worse because you're still hurt and now you've lost a friend?

If you find that what you intended and what you got don't match up all that well, take some time to think about how you could have approached things differently. For example: When you approached your friend, were you calm and respectful or were you angry and accusatory? Did you listen to her response with an open heart and mind or did you interrupt her and demand an apology?

By doing this exercise from time to time, you can help ensure that your intentions and actions are in better alignment. And if through the exercise you find an opportunity to correct your behavior, then be brave and do it! Call that friend and apologize for your angry tone. Explain that her friendship is so important to you that it felt particularly hurtful when she stepped on your feelings, even though you know she didn't mean to. Then see what happens. There's no guarantee you'll get what you want, but you'll have a much better chance. Plus, you'll get to feel better about yourself and your part in what happened.

4

THE ENERGY EXCHANGE

"If you could only sense how important you are to the lives of those you meet;
how important you can be to the people you may never even dream of. There is
something of yourself that you leave at every meeting with another person."

MISTER (FRED) ROGERS, *The World According to Mister Rogers*[1]

Micro-gestures have the power to change people because they allow us to put a different energy into the world. The act of giving is as important as the object you give, if not more so. GAF is not just about the plate of food you make for someone, or the time you spend reading to someone at the hospital, or the favor you do for your injured neighbor, or whatever your offering may be. The act of giving carries with it a whole range of gifts that are less tangible but no less important.

For example, when you give to someone, you're letting that person know that you see her. You're also showing the person that you believe him worthy of your time and attention as well as the object you're giving him. GAF conveys your acknowledgment, consideration, and respect for the other person—the same feelings that all of us want from our interactions with others, no matter how much we might already have in terms of material goods.

This is why, as you start your micro-gestures, you want to make sure you're being intentional, not just about *what* you give to people, but about *how* you give it. I once saw a young guy on a street corner who was collecting signatures for some environmental cause. I could tell he really cared about the issue because of how much he knew about it. As I was waiting for a friend, I watched him have an in-depth conversation with an older man who was testing him with questions: the guy had a thorough answer for every one, and he was glad to give it. But then the interaction came to an end, and it was time to approach someone new. The young guy looked around, spotted a woman heading his way, and rushed right up to her, shoving his clipboard in her face. The woman, who was wearing earbuds and hadn't seen him coming, dodged him and kept on walking.

The guy was clearly irritated about being ignored. "I guess you don't care about our world then!" he yelled after her.

To master the micro-gesture, it helps to look at all interactions between people as an exchange of energy. You can see the energy at work in the moment that unfolded in front of me. The young guy appeared to be a good person. He wasn't trying to hurt or harass the woman he approached. In fact, he had a noble purpose for wanting to talk to her. But there was a problem, which was that these weren't the things that came through energetically as he approached her. The guy was so focused on his mission that he forgot to be considerate of the person he was appealing to. And that lack of consideration was surely what the woman was reacting to when she dodged him. I don't think she had any idea what he wanted from her. She just knew that he'd startled her. And instead of apologizing for it, the guy yelled after her as if she were to blame.

ENERGY EXCHANGE: A DEFINITION

The back-and-forth flow of energy that happens whenever two (or more) people encounter one another.

Passion is a good thing, but it matters how you present that passion to others if you want anything good to come of it. It's the energy that sparks between people that makes the difference between a positive experience and a negative one, between a loving experience and a not-so-loving one. It's like the old adage says: "It's not just what you say, but how you say it that counts." The same can be said about *how* you love others and *how* you give to them.

ENERGY AND EMOTION

Later in this chapter, we'll talk about different ways to be intentional about the energy you bring to an exchange, but before we do that, we need to talk about why this can be so tricky. It's our emotions that can complicate things. Our energetic state is often fueled by emotion, and that can make our energy unpredictable.

As a general rule, whatever energy you bring into an interaction is the same energy that you'll get back in the end. That's not always going to be true, but most of the time it will be. This means that if you're bringing negative feelings into your interaction with someone, you're likely to get a negative reaction in return. For example, think about what typically happens if you're rude to someone on the bus or in line at the DMV. The person is likely to be rude back. On the other hand, a friendly word to a stranger or a smile as you pass someone on the street is often returned in kind.

You can imagine the kind of feelings that might lead to an energetic state that others will reject or react to poorly, whether or not they know you well: anxiousness, insecurity, sadness, anger, hopelessness, to name a few. No one likes to feel these things, so when we sense them in others, the reaction tends to be less than positive.

Fear is another common feeling that gets in the way of loving exchanges. Not long ago I was being interviewed on a podcast about our work at LOM, and one of the interviewer's very first questions was about fear: "Aren't you afraid of people when you're down on Skid Row?"

She was a young woman living in a big city, so I understood where she was coming from. We all want to stay safe, and fear is common when we set out to do something new or encounter something that we don't fully understand and can't control—like homelessness, addiction, or mental illness (to name a few). But while fear is natural, it can also serve as an excuse for not trying new things or not moving forward in our lives. There's a difference between protecting ourselves from harm and making decisions based on fear. The latter can cause us to miss opportunities to grow, expand, and create better lives for ourselves.

This doesn't mean that we don't protect ourselves by locking our doors at night or making sure we have an exit strategy if we're going on a blind date. But it does mean acknowledging that much of what we fear is not what we really need to be afraid of. It means understanding that what we feel often stems from past experiences rather than our experience of what's happening right here, right now.

Look, we're all human. We're all going to experience fear from time to time. And anger. And insecurity. And unworthiness. And everything else that the human experience encompasses. There's no use pretending otherwise. There's no point in trying to suppress these feelings either.

What we can do is work on becoming more mindful of how we show up to different situations and how our feelings affect both us and the situations we're in. The more awareness we have, the more we'll be able to choose where to place our focus. I go to a lot of wellness conferences and speak in front of a lot of people interested in spirituality and health. I'm often surprised in these communities how much energy people put toward their pain. Even in spaces where people are actively searching for mental, spiritual, and physical wellness, those same people often lean into their pain. That seems to be the default for some, while others will do everything possible to avoid even acknowledging their pain. Either way, if we're not careful, our emotions—especially our negative ones—will be happy to run the show for us.

While it's true that we all have negative or painful experiences that affect us, it's equally true that we all have good experiences to draw on as well. Just think about how many wonderful things happen in our lives without us having to do anything to make them happen. The sun shines on us. The flowers bloom for us. We have been given life, and we have been given love. And that's just the beginning. So why do we often choose to place more focus on the things that weigh us down and cloud our energy rather than the things that lift us up? We do have a choice in the matter, and a greater awareness of our feelings and how they affect us will allow us to make more empowering choices.

❤ HEARTWORK ❤
CHECK IN WITH YOUR FEELINGS

Make an effort to check in with your feelings regularly so you become more comfortable with their full range. The more comfortable you are with your feelings, the less likely it is that one will take you by surprise. I like to do this every morning before I start my day. Instead of getting up and checking my phone, I make a point of checking in with myself first. I call it my "morning check-in time," and for me, it works best if I sit in silence while I focus on how I'm feeling. Others may prefer to write in a journal or use some other method to check in with themselves.

During your morning check-in, ask yourself the following questions:

How am I feeling right now?

How might those feelings affect my energy or actions as I move through my day?

How would I like to be feeling right now?

When you do this, you might find that some of the things you're feeling aren't so pretty. You don't have to beat yourself up over it, and you don't have to wait until you find some perfect state of grace before attempting to interact with others in a loving and giving way. We're just trying to build our awareness here of how we function, and why, so we're better able to choose how we show up in the world.

PRACTICING ACTS OF NON-RESISTANCE

If we allow our emotions to dictate our energy, then we're bound to miss out on opportunities and have fewer positive encounters with people. To avoid that, we all need to practice being open vessels, ready to take in an experience as it unfolds. This means approaching situations with a neutral energy whenever possible, instead of with feelings the situation itself hasn't yet merited. It means doing our best to show up without preconceived ideas, expectations, or biases. I mentioned this to the young woman who asked me during her podcast interview if I was afraid of people on Skid Row. If we can put ourselves in a neutral state before we approach someone, then I believe we actually have a better chance of picking up on the person's energy and being forewarned if that person means us harm. In other words, we respond better when our emotions aren't clouding our judgment.

This is something I learned from my dad, who, while not my biological father, chose to play that role in my life. One day, while I was staying with my grandmother, I missed him so much that I called him up to ask him if he would be my dad. He and my birth mom weren't even married at the time, and he was only twenty years old, but he said, "Of course." He adopted me soon after, and he was the stabilizing force for me at home before I was old enough to leave my birth mother behind. Now he's a surgeon, and that stabilizing energy is something he makes use of every day. After all, a surgeon can't freak out when a patient's heartbeat becomes erratic while she's on the operating table. Being calm and nonreactive to triggers is crucial to his work because it allows him to process what's happening and determine how best to proceed. If he wasn't able to do that, people could die.

This is an "act of non-resistance." It means making a conscious effort *not* to resist the truth of what's in front of you. If we can learn how to accept people and situations as they are, even if they're difficult or unpleasant, then there's so much more we can take from them and so much more we can do to affect them in a positive way. To stand in our own power and hear someone out, even if that person is yelling or being unkind, is an act of non-resistance. To bear witness to someone else's pain and suffering, even though we'd rather turn away, is an act of non-resistance too.

I often think about why my dad became a master of this. When he was growing up in Philadelphia, shootings would take place just outside his bedroom window. He couldn't do anything about what was happening around him, but he still found a useful way to respond. He didn't get his own gun or add to the violence. He didn't run to the window to watch, thereby risking getting shot himself. He didn't hide under his covers or refuse to go outside ever again. Instead, he took up reading. He would find a relatively safe corner of his room to curl up in and then he would disappear into books. As he told me, "I would read so I could travel far away from what was happening outside."

Resisting unpleasant feelings—whether we're talking about sadness, fear, shame, or discomfort—is a pretty typical response for most of us. We tend to instinctively fight back or run away—the fight-or-flight response—when confronted with something we don't want to feel. We put up walls. We protect our hearts. In fact, many of us spend quite a lot of time protecting ourselves from situations that aren't really going to hurt us. But if we want to have more positive and more meaningful interactions with people—whether we're talking about strangers or our closest friends and family—there needs to be more non-resistance. There needs to be more silence. We need to give ourselves more time and space to listen and observe, and then reflect on what we've witnessed, rather than react instinctively or based on emotion. That's what will allow us to be more intentional about the energy we bring to a situation. And, as we'll talk about in the next chapter, it's also what will allow us to be more open to the energy that comes back to us.

Engaging in acts of non-resistance doesn't have to be as difficult as it sounds. We can start by asking ourselves if relying on our knee-jerk reactions to situations, just because that's our habit, is what we really want. We can ask ourselves if those knee-jerk reactions have benefited us: Have they made our relationships stronger or weaker? Have they made us feel stronger or weaker?

If our reactions aren't benefiting us, then we can choose to try another way. Rather than being reactive, we can create more space in which to form considered responses by doing the following:

1) No matter what's happening (unless you're in immediate danger and you need to run for your life, which, let's

face it, doesn't happen all that often), take a pause and choose not to react. Feel what you're feeling, but choose not to react to those feelings for the moment.

2) Look and listen in silence. Make an effort to pick up on what's going on around you as much as possible.

3) Observe the energy that's flowing: your own as well as that of the other person or people near you. And take as long as you need. Together these three steps may take one minute for some people while others may need to pause for five to ten minutes to get their bearings.

4) Now proceed with intention.

These four simple steps will put you in a nonreactive state. As often as possible, this is where you'll want to be as you practice your micro-gestures. Before you approach someone, you can take a moment to run through these steps in your mind. You can also do something similar after the interaction has finished in order to process the experience: stop, look and listen, observe the energy, and then intentionally reflect on what happened and how it felt.

Most of us are moving so quickly through life, juggling so many tasks and responsibilities, that it may feel foreign at first to slow down in this way. But it's such a valuable skill that I suggest you practice it outside of your micro-gestures and outside of the more stressful or triggering moments in your life. For example, the next time you're at a café by yourself, sitting in a park, or waiting in line, stop and look around. Watch how people interact with each other and see what you can pick up on. Even if you can't hear what people are saying, there's a lot you can gather from just being a calm, nonreactive witness. Are the people you're watching acting in an animated or a subdued way? Looking one another in the eye or not? What's happening with their facial expressions? Their body language? You can often guess

ACTS OF NON-RESISTANCE: A DEFINITION

The ability to *not* react right away to a situation, to resist the impulse to follow the emotions of or be triggered by the moment. Instead, allowing the moment to unfold in front of you and witnessing it without judgment so you can process it and respond with intention.

what sort of relationship two people have and whether their interaction is positive, negative, or neutral without ever meeting them or hearing a word they're saying.

I believe we're naturally more sensitive and in tune with one another than we give ourselves credit for. We just have to put up our mental antennas and give ourselves the time and space needed to pick up on what's happening around us. You may have to do this deliberately at first, but the more you practice it, the more it will become second nature.

LOVE IS IN THE DETAILS

So how do we go about giving to others with the right kind of energy? Sure, our emotions can complicate things, but we're aware of that fact and we're trying our best. We don't need to wait for some fundamental change to take place in our personalities before we start our micro-gestures. We just need to work on making some small, conscious shifts. In fact, the difference between a positive interaction and a negative one can often be found in the details.

I once had a woman tell me she wasn't going to do any more micro-gestures because when she'd last tried to feed someone, the man had rejected outright the food she'd offered him. "He was so rude about it," she said, imitating for me how he'd waved her away with his hand. It had obviously hurt her feelings pretty badly.

Immediately I wondered if there weren't ways she might think differently and more generously about what had happened. First, I don't think it makes a lot of sense to deny everyone else your gifts, or to deny yourself the chance to be giving, just because one person rejected what you had to offer. Think about it the same way you might think about love: just because you have one bad relationship doesn't mean you give up on trying to find the love in your life. Some of us may shut down when we're hurt, but we also know it's not a very healthy thing to do long term. When it comes to GAF, not every experience is going to be great. Of course, you could say that about any kind of experience. There's never going to be a one hundred percent guarantee of positive return with anything you do in life. But I know from experience that with giving, especially when you do it mindfully and with intention, the good experiences far outnumber the bad ones. So I asked her: "What about the other times you've made food for people? Weren't people receptive to what you gave them?"

It turned out that this was the first time she'd tried this kind of micro-gesture, and because of her experience, she hadn't tried it a second time. That made me wonder about *how* she had gone about offering her gift, which prompted a few more questions: How did she greet the man? What did she say to him about why she was there? Was she smiling? How did she feel when she approached him?

As we talked more about it, it gradually became clear that she'd walked up to a man who'd been napping against a building and woken him up by trying to hand him a wrapped-up package of food. She hadn't told him who she was. She hadn't told him what she was giving him. She couldn't remember if she'd been smiling or not (which means she probably wasn't), and she admitted that what she had felt most of all as she was doing this was nervousness about talking to a stranger.

It wasn't the ideal way to approach someone. Not surprisingly, she got a less than ideal reaction. But she also got an opportunity to learn some key things about how the energy exchange works.

I suggested that she try again, only this time, before doing anything, spend some time thinking about how she'd like to be approached by a stranger. Then apply that to the person in front of her. It helped her to have a kind of checklist of things to think through that might affect how she's received, so we broke down some of the elements that make up any encounter.

Whether or not our love and good intentions come through to someone else is often in the details—for example, how we greet someone. Following are some of those details that she considered, and I encourage you to consider each of them as well when you offer your own micro-gestures.

Greetings

The woman I spoke to wasn't alone in rushing past this step. At LOM, we work with a lot of volunteers who are new to the work we do. In the beginning, it surprised me how often I would see one of them walk right up to someone on Skid Row to offer their help without first saying hello. That kind of abruptness can be intimidating to someone who is wary of strangers, which is most people living on the streets—most people anywhere, really. It can also be off-putting to someone looking for acknowledgment and kindness.

"Hi, I'm [insert your name here]," said with a smile, is a good and simple place to start. I personally like to include a term of endearment so that people feel straight off where I'm coming from. "Hi love" or "Hey boo" are my most common greetings when I'm on Skid Row, but there's no one right thing to say. You just have to remember that while you know you have good intentions, the other person does not, so think about how best to come across as open and friendly from the very first word.

Attitude

It's important to check in with your feelings before you go up to someone because your feelings can subconsciously affect your attitude. Are you nervous? Afraid? Intimidated? Then chances are the person you're approaching will pick up on that energy and feel ill at ease as well. Take a deep breath to calm your energy. Remind yourself why you're there and what feeling you want to convey. Focusing on that can help mitigate some of the awkwardness of a first encounter.

Then, I find it works best to keep it simple and go for a casual approach. After your initial greeting, you might ask the person's name. You can explain what you're doing there and what you're offering in an informal way. You might say something like: "I have some extra food and I wondered if you might be hungry," or "It's so hot out today, I thought you might like a drink," or "I'm going into this store and I wondered if you might need anything," or "I saw you over here and I wondered if you could use some help."

The idea isn't to surprise or intimidate anyone, or to force something on someone that the person doesn't want. Instead, you want to make the person feel comfortable, so think about how you would approach someone you're already comfortable with, like a friend or a neighbor, and imitate that.

Language

Words carry energy, which means the words we choose matter. For example, I don't call LOM a "charity" because I believe it has become a dirty word. When someone thinks of themselves as doing "charitable work," they tend to have in the back of their minds this idea that they are up on some higher plane, and the people they are helping are down below receiving their largesse. I call this the "savior complex," and it's the exact opposite of what we want in our energy exchange, which is for everyone to feel like they're on the same level. It's important to remember that GAF is a gift you give to yourself as much as others—if not more so—so there is no "higher" or "lower" person in the exchange.

Similarly, at LOM we don't call the people we serve "the homeless." We use words like "street family" or "wildflowers." The words you choose reflect what you believe, and we believe the people we give a f♥ck about are more than just homeless people—a lot more. That term describes their living situation but nothing about who they are, which is why what we try to do most of all is learn people's names and use them. Calling someone Primo or Big Joe or Asher feels a lot different than saying "that homeless man."

These are just a couple of examples to help you start thinking about how to be more conscious and intentional about the words you use when you're giving. One of the best ways to think about it is to imagine whether you'd want to be on the receiving end of whatever descriptive word it is you're thinking of using. Also think about how the language you're using changes the way you feel about the people you interact with or the gifts you're giving. Do you think about the people you give to as "needy" or "charity cases"? Or could you use words like *sharing, caring, serving,* or *connecting* to describe the role you might play in the exchange?

Touch

Another positive way to take part in the energy exchange is through touch. While many of us at LOM regularly give our wildflowers hugs or reach out and grab their hands when we see them, we often get volunteers whose eyes go wide when they notice this. The people we serve don't have easy access to showers, it's true, but that doesn't mean they are any less deserving of a little human contact. It's a basic need. Depriving people of touch is depriving them of a key expression of love.

I have to admit, this particular expression didn't come naturally to me. My friend Shaianne once brought her grandmother for a visit, and when we were hugging hello, her grandmother said to me (in the nicest possible way): "Your hugs are terrible. You gotta get better at hugs." I laughed, but she was serious. She gently explained to me that my arms were too limp and I let go too quickly. In contrast, she hugged like she was never letting you go, and you just felt her warmth radiating through you. I knew she was telling me this out of love, so I took her advice and practiced until I got more comfortable with hugging.

In order to practice, I started asking people when I met them if they wanted a hug, and it became obvious pretty quickly that there are lots of people out there who want more human contact in their lives. Of course, I didn't want to force a hug on anyone, so I always asked first. I had such good results that I still do this. When I meet someone new, I usually say: "Can I have a hug? It's more for me than it is for you." The answer I get is almost always an enthusiastic, "Yes, I want one too!"

WHY I GIVE A F♥CK . . .

"I can get really down on myself sometimes, and sometimes I look around and get really down about the world. But I've found that the best way to feel better about myself is to stop thinking so much about myself. It may sound counterintuitive, but I think that the best way to heal is to try to heal others."

REID
writer, age 49

Touch is uncomfortable for some people, so it may be something you want to work up to. When my friend Emily moved to Los Angeles and started working with Lunch On Me, we took her with us to Arizona, where I was speaking at a conference. By that point, people who knew about our organization were used to our open-hug policy, but Emily didn't know that. She was on her own, in a shop across the street from the conference center, wearing her Lunch On Me T-shirt, when people started walking up to her out of nowhere (or so it felt to her) to say hello and give her a hug. She wasn't a touchy-feely person by nature, so she was a bit taken aback by it at first. But after a short while, it started to feel natural to her too. The value of touch was something that she and I both had to learn as adults, but I think we're both really glad that we did.

After you've been doing micro-gestures for a while, you may find that there are certain people that you're helping on a regular basis, and it feels natural to greet them with an embrace. Or you may find that you're just more comfortable with people in general and able to develop a quick rapport because of all the practice you've had. Keep in mind that this kind of loving expression doesn't just have to be about hugs. It can be a squeeze of someone's hand, a pat on the back, a kiss on the cheek—whatever you and the other person both feel good about.

THE GOLDEN RULE OF GIVING: GIVE WHAT YOU'D WANT TO RECEIVE

Just as the words we choose carry energy and reflect what we believe, so do the things we choose to give. When you think about what you have to offer someone, are you thinking about what someone would be happy to receive? Or are you thinking about what you have that you don't want anymore and how this could be a chance to unload it?

Energetically, there's a huge difference between the two, and you're fooling yourself if you think that people on the receiving end of the exchange can't tell the difference. For example, you'd be amazed at the amount of public dollars that go toward feeding people in need food you wouldn't dream of eating yourself. When I first started Lunch On Me, there was a man on Skid Row named Scotty who came up to me one day to tell me how much he hoped we'd stick around: "I can tell by the food you serve that you really care."

I asked him what he meant, and he pointed to a nonprofit with headquarters down the block that also served food to the community, but it was mostly processed foods and cheap products, not the kind of fresh, healthy food that we offer. "I call tell by what they serve us that they hate us," Scotty said, whispering as if it were a secret. "What they got makes me feel sick so I don't even eat it anymore. I'd rather go hungry."

I think most of us inherently understand what he was talking about, but sometimes we forget to apply that understanding in unfamiliar situations. In our personal lives, we know that food is about more than just sustenance. We eat to make ourselves feel better. When we're sick or unhappy, it's often our mom's comfort food that we want the most. When we have something to celebrate, we share some of the best food that we can afford with our friends and family. We would never invite people over for a birthday party and serve old, expired junk that we found in the back of our pantry. So why is that old, expired junk good enough for the local food drive? Why is it good enough for you to give?

This goes back to the idea we talked about in chapter 2, about being mindful of the stories we tell ourselves and how we truly view other people, because those feelings come through. In the back of your mind, is there some version of this thought: "I'm giving this to people for free, so they should just be happy with what I give them." If so, it's likely that the people you give to will pick up on that energy.

We need to ask ourselves: Are we really giving if it doesn't feel like a gift to the person receiving it? Are we really giving if it's not what the person needs or wants? Have you ever had a partner or spouse give you something for your birthday or a holiday that you just knew was more about his or her needs, or your family's needs, than your own? It doesn't feel great when that happens. Similarly, if we give what we want to unload, then that's really more about us and our needs than it is about the other person.

Another way to approach the question is to ask ourselves whether being in need of help makes someone inherently less worthy than someone else. It's useful to remember that we all have needs that go unsatisfied at times: a need for love, for recognition, for respect, for understanding, for empathy, to name a few. Some people have more tangible needs—like food, shelter, medicine, or other resources—but even those things get all tangled up with the same needs we all have and can relate to. Just like my friend on Skid Row said: some of the food he was served made him feel hated, and none of us want to feel that way.

It has always been my policy at LOM to never serve anything to anyone that I wouldn't eat myself because I know that for all of us, food is about more than just food. Serving a warm, nourishing, and tasty meal is an act of caring, an act of sharing, an act of love. On Skid Row, food is my gift. It's a personal gesture to show people that I love them, because love is something we all need and something that I need to express.

The same applies no matter what kind of gift you're choosing to give, so remember to ask yourself these kinds of questions. Is what you're giving something that you would be happy to get? Are you giving it in a way that you'd be happy to receive it? Because if you wouldn't want it, why would anyone else?

❤ HEARTWORK ❤

Before you offer something to someone else, first ask yourself:

Is what I'm giving something that I would be happy to get if I were that person?

Am I prepared to give it in a way that I would be happy to receive it?

OPEN YOURSELF UP TO THE ENERGY OF GIVING

One of the basic rules of the energy exchange is that you get what you give. Every act of giving and caring, sharing and loving is part of a universal exchange. This isn't just about you giving something and someone else taking it, but too many people see it that way. It's that way of thinking that has kept us stuck in unhealthy patterns; it's why we have so many problems that persist, or worsen, despite all the resources our society has poured into them.

So much of our giving is done with the wrong kind of energy. We give expecting something in return, even if it's just a thank you. We give expecting to be praised for our "good work." I've even seen volunteers take selfies with the people we feed so they can post them on Instagram as if to say: "Look how awesome I was today!" When this happens, I gently remind them that they can't show up like that in this space. I think we could all make more of an effort to put down our phones and get off social media so that we can connect more directly with the people right in front of us. If we can be more mindful of what's happening in the moment, right now, then we'll be better able to let go of our expectations and open ourselves up to what can be a truly joyful experience.

Giving puts you in a position to receive because you are energetically participating in the exchange. People may not realize it at first, but deep down many of them are longing to take part. You see it in small gestures all the time. It's in the "take a book, leave a book" kiosks people put up on their lawns to share books with their neighbors. I saw it at my local yoga studio the other day where someone left a basket of fruits from her garden for others to sample. It's why people on Skid Row save up their change to buy forks or water bottles that they can donate to LOM when they come to get their meals—because they want to be a part of the exchange too.

We talked earlier in this chapter about the negative feelings that can cloud your energy and sometimes make your giving less successful than you intended. But there is another aspect of giving that can be truly powerful if you let it: If you can stay mindful and intentional, giving can be a way of working through the difficult things we all experience in our lives. If you're feeling rejected, you can go out and offer your gifts to be accepted. If you're feeling disconnected, you can go out and intentionally connect with someone in a positive and loving way. If you're feeling disempowered, you can go out and make a real difference in someone's life—and what could be more empowering than that? Sometimes it can be hard to be kind to ourselves, but extending our kindness to others can help us feel better about ourselves. When we can give to others what we want for ourselves, we often find what we need in the process.

Along the way, try to be mindful about projecting your negative feelings or energy onto others. And if you do, don't beat yourself up; simply correct your behavior and try again. If you can do that, this can be a great space to work through things that are holding you back in your life while also getting a chance to do something positive for others.

This chapter has been mostly about the energy you bring to the exchange, but once you have opened yourself up and started to participate in it, there will also be the energy you get back. Energetically, being a joyful giver can come back to you so fast. People may not understand that at first, but it doesn't take long to learn if you're open to the lesson, and that's what the next chapter is about.

5

LESSONS FROM SKID ROW

"Let me seek, O Lord
not so much to be understood, but to understand;
Not to be loved, but to love.
For it is in giving that one receives."

FROM "THE PRAYER OF ST. FRANCIS" *by Anonymous[1]*

Taking part in the energy exchange means being conscious of what you give and how you give it, like we talked about in the last chapter. But it also means something else. It means being conscious of what comes back to you—of the gifts you receive by taking part. You may be offering a plate of food or your time, but what you get in return is often something that, though less tangible, is even more profound. I mean that truly. What comes back to you in exchange for your service to others can be as big as a lesson about life, a realization about yourself, a reminder of what really matters in this world. GAF puts you in a position to receive some amazing gifts, if you can only open yourself up to notice and embrace them.

In this chapter I want to talk about some of the amazing gifts I've received by being of service on Skid Row. Of course, not everyone will get a chance to visit Skid Row, so I use my experience only as an example, as a reminder that the spiritual lessons we're looking for can be found anywhere—while you're watching your kids in the park, when you're in a meeting at work, while you're walking down the street, when you're packed together on public transportation, really anywhere. (Just as an aside: subways, buses, and airplanes are great places to contemplate how humanity works, especially since you can't just leave when something makes you feel uncomfortable.)

The gifts I've been given on Skid Row have most often come in the form of life lessons. You will, no doubt, encounter similar lessons as you perform your micro-gestures, and even discover some that are your own. The main point here is really to get into the habit of opening your eyes up wide to look for those gifts. And then allowing them in to change you for the better.

EVERYONE HAS SOMETHING TO TEACH US

I talked before about how we often have more gifts than we realize to share with people and make a difference in their lives. The reverse is also true. Everyone, no matter who they are or what circumstances they're living in, has something good to offer us, something important to teach us. That has become more and more clear to me the longer I've done this work.

This is why it's so important to pause and take note of what's happening energetically as we serve others. We don't want those gifts to pass us by.

Practicing your acts of non-resistance and maintaining a neutral energy will help put you in a better position to pick up on such things. Once our antennas are up and attuned to the people around us, we'll find that lessons about life are happening all around us. During my time serving people on Skid Row, I've been reminded that those who have suffered the most also have gone on some of the most profound spiritual journeys as a result of that suffering. That's why they have so much to teach us.

You might be surprised to learn that some of the most gracious people I've ever met live on Skid Row. It happens regularly that people will come to get a meal from us and want to offer something in return. One man named Kenneth likes to bring his artwork, which he does on recycled cardboard boxes, to give to our volunteers. Because one of our biggest costs at LOM is for plates and eating utensils (things that aren't routinely donated by grocery stores because their shelf life isn't limited), many of our street family save up their change to buy these items for us. When they can't do that, they save their utensils from a previous meal so they don't have to use another set.

We give out as much extra food as we can at each meal service so that our street family has something when we're not there—loaves of bread, packages of crackers, or other organic packaged foods—but when we run through our supply, some people are always left unlucky. Every time I'm on Skid Row, I see people sharing what they have because every person there knows what it's like to go without. They can empathize with the feeling so they want to do something about it. The attitude of "I have something you need today, and you might have something I need tomorrow, so let's share" is simply a way of life on Skid Row.

The lesson of generosity is also one I'm confronted with frequently. It seems like it shouldn't be the case, but the people who have the least are often the ones who are the most generous. And I'm not the only one who has witnessed that fact: research shows that, on average, people who have less give a greater percentage of what they have than those who have the most.[2] It's a reminder that how much we give to others has little to do with how much we can spare, and a lot to do with how we think about people specifically and the world in general.

Beyond that, living in the world today comes with a whole new set of issues the likes of which our grandparents never had to worry about. Like the fact that, if we're not careful, we can get overstimulated so easily. Think about how many devices you interact with every day. A phone, surely, and probably also a computer and a television set. Maybe even a tablet and/or a smart watch. If you have the notifications turned on, then one or more of these devices may be ringing or pinging or blaring at you from the moment you get up in the morning, or even while you're trying to sleep if you're not good about turning them off. I recently read a hotel listing that boasted about having phone lock boxes in every room so that guests could force themselves to relax and enjoy their surroundings. If we want to find quiet, we have to consciously construct a context for that to happen by removing ourselves from all these different means of input.

Not so on Skid Row. While we have to actively carve out time for solitude (and sometimes even pay top dollar for it at wellness retreats or meditation centers), many of the people there have been in solitude for years. They have so much time to spend with themselves that they inherently know how to just be. Isn't that an enviable quality?

People living on the streets also know how to just be with each other. So many live in tents on the sidewalk or packed together in shelters, which means they have no walls to hide behind, no doors they can close between one another, no cars they can drive off in alone. As a result, most of the people I've met have had to learn how to get along.

In other words, they know how to do things like empathize and apologize. One day my colleagues and I were setting up tables to serve food on a street corner downtown. As often happens, people started lining up early so they could be the first to eat. Among them were a couple of women, both of whom we'd served before. I don't know what started it, but they began yelling angrily at each other until one of them had had enough and stalked away. Butterfly was her name, and I didn't see her again until the next day when she came running up to me as I was unloading food from my car.

"I'm so sorry about yesterday," she said. "I was just really tired and hungry, and when Joselyn bumped into me like that, I lost it. Everyone is always so happy when you show up, and I wouldn't want to do anything to make you feel like you don't want to come back. I'm really sorry to have disrespected you. It won't happen again."

I was touched by her apology and impressed that she'd given it so freely when I hadn't even thought I deserved one. After all, the altercation hadn't amounted to much, and it hadn't affected me directly. So I told her how much I appreciated what she'd said and then mentioned that the person she should probably be apologizing to was Joselyn.

"I tried!" she said, looking genuinely distressed. "I've been trying to find her all day, but she hasn't been around!"

I was kind of amazed. I've dated people from whom I've failed to pry apologies for doing much worse. If we could all learn how to admit our mistakes and express our remorse so freely and genuinely, imagine how much nicer the world would be.

❤ HEARTWORK ❤

Take a moment to remember the teachers in your life, especially the unexpected ones. For example, maybe you had an algebra teacher in school from whom you expected to learn about equations, but who also taught you a valuable lesson about self-esteem or forgiving yourself. Or maybe someone you sat next to on the bus had some wise words for you one day. Think about who has helped you open your mind and heart and write down their names and what they taught you.

If you're still in touch with these people or able to track them down, consider writing them a note of thanks for what they gave you.

REMEMBER THE GIFTS WE ALREADY HAVE

I was once in a car service, talking with the driver, when we discovered something unexpected. The driver, a woman about my age, had asked me what I do for a living, so I was telling her about our work on Skid Row. That's when she mentioned that she thought her sister lived there. As we got to talking more about it, it turned out that her sister and I knew each other.

This woman and her sister had lost contact some years earlier. She didn't tell me what had happened between them, but she was curious about her sister so I told her what I knew. Among the things I mentioned was that her sister wrote poetry and had shared some of it with me.

"I think she's really very talented," I told my driver, to which she replied: "Wow, I didn't even know she wrote."

Not long after that experience, my colleague Venus came to work very upset because a woman she'd made a connection with on Skid Row had disappeared. Venus had been asking around about the woman, and while no one knew for sure, word was that she'd died. Caring can be tough. It can be hard to make a connection with someone, and even when one is made, it can be hard to keep it. We all lose people sometimes. But the loss of this woman made me think of my driver and her sister. The moments I'd had with her sister, talking about life and hearing her poetry, were special ones, but they were also ones that her sister could have been having with her. When we parted ways that day, I gave the driver my contact information. "If you want to get in touch with your sister, I can help," I said, but I've yet to hear from her.

As hard as it is, when we lose someone on Skid Row, it serves as a reminder of how important it is to take advantage of the time we have with each other. While I'm not naïve about these things, and I certainly understand that what comes between people can be large and overwhelming, I still wondered what would have happened if my driver had learned that day that her sister was no longer living nearby. I wondered how she would have reacted if I'd had to tell her that I'd known her sister once but she had passed, and there was no longer an opportunity to connect with her. It also made me think about my own siblings and how long it had been since I'd connected with them. I went home and called all seven of them that very night just to check in.

Ask yourself: *What people or things in my life have I been over-looking or taking for granted?*

It's often the people closest to us or the things we've relied on the longest that we forget to appreciate. So think hard about your answer and look close . . . at your family, your oldest friend, your home, and your community.

The point of this exercise isn't to make you feel bad about yourself. We all take things for granted from time to time. Instead, make a point of acknowledging it and doing something to shift toward a more intentional frame of mind. If you've been taking your spouse for granted, for example, what can you do today to show your appreciation?

Ask yourself this question from time to time as a reminder of just how much good you already have in your life.

GRATITUDE IS A BYPRODUCT OF SERVICE

Among the lessons I've seen people embrace by performing their micro-gestures is the true meaning of gratitude. Gratitude has become a big idea in certain circles these days, and a lot has been written about research showing that a focus on gratitude has real benefits for people in terms of their mental and physical well-being.[3] This is probably why the practice of gratitude journaling has become so popular. You can even buy gratitude journals at your local bookstore ready for you to fill in the blanks about what makes you feel lucky today.

I have to admit that I have a bit of a bone to pick with the gratitude journalers of the world. It's not that I disagree with the research or the idea that gratitude can be a powerful force. It's that I think the idea of gratitude, perhaps because it has become so popular, is too often misunderstood.

I don't believe that gratitude is about sitting in your room and saying thanks so only your walls can hear you. I don't believe it's something that should remain in the pages of a journal. I don't believe it's something you can find on a bracelet or in an Instagram quote. These can be good ways to remind yourself to be thankful, but they're not enough. That's because gratitude isn't meant to be passive. "God is a verb," as Paulo Coelho once said in an interview with Oprah Winfrey about his bestselling book, *The Alchemist*.[4] I believe that gratitude, too, needs to be treated as an action.

In fact, we used to talk about gratitude in terms of *giving thanks,* which makes it sound so much more active, instead of merely *being thankful.* Rightly so, because I believe gratitude is something you should *do*, not something you merely think or feel or write about. This means you can't just read in the news about the hurricane that devastated a town or the drug problem that plagues a community and feel thankful that you're removed from it and safe. You can't just walk by people in need and feel sorry for their suffering and grateful that you're not in the same position. True gratitude is more than just a feeling. It's the expression of that feeling through action—the action of serving others. To truly be grateful, you have to act gratefully.

It's a bit like that old philosophical question about whether, if a tree falls in the woods and no one hears it, did it really fall? By the same token, if you love someone but you never express that love, either verbally or through your actions, can you really call it love? If you're grateful for what you have but never extend that gratitude to others, then are you truly living a grateful life?

When we mindfully show our appreciation for what we have through the action of serving others, then gratitude is the result. It's the byproduct of that service, and there's really no other way to get it. We live in a world that loves shortcuts. If there's a faster, easier, simpler way to get something done, then we're all over it. People write about "life hacks" as if they're going to save us, but some things can't be hacked. I believe that gratitude is one of them.

In the energy exchange, there's a dynamic between people made up of living, breathing energy that flows back and forth. When that energy stops moving, it dies. Gratitude has an energy behind it too, but I believe that energy dies, or at least atrophies, when we keep it confined to our thoughts and prayers or the pages of our journal. Even sharing grateful thoughts on social media—which I highly encourage as an antidote to all the complaints and judgments that tend to be put on display—is not the same as allowing our gratitude to inspire us to act on behalf of others. Because it's so often relegated to contexts like these, gratitude is really in danger of losing its meaning.

I was once in a yoga class that was winding down on a hot day when I witnessed a missed opportunity to really live gratitude. We were all sitting in Lotus Position with the lights dimmed and the door open so the breeze could flow through the studio. Soft music was playing in the background and our hands were pressed together at our hearts as we whispered our "namastes." Just then a man, who appeared to be suffering from mental illness, walked in through the open door to say hello and ask, "What are you all doing in here?" He was friendly enough, but the reaction was immediate. The people closest to him scattered while others turned away or shook their heads. No one answered him. I meant to, but I didn't gather my thoughts quickly enough. The teacher rushed over to tell him to leave, pushing him out the door and closing it behind him.

It was as if everyone in the room had forgotten what they'd been doing right before the man walked in. Yoga classes often end with the students saying *namaste* as an expression of gratitude for the experience they just had, the teacher who guided them through it, and the fellow students they shared it with. But it's also generally considered to have spiritual connotations, to be a conscious acknowledgment of another person's soul, of the divine light that resides in all of us. Some literally translate namaste from Sanskrit to mean: "The light in me acknowledges the light in you."

I guess my fellow classmates decided that not everyone was worthy of a namaste. I don't mean to be overly harsh. I get why people were frightened, as they often are by mental illness, or turned off by the disruption when they were in the midst of a peaceful moment. But if we'd all taken a moment to simply notice this man (an act of non-resistance), I think it would have quickly become clear that he meant us no harm. He was just curious and, I think, lonely. It seemed like what he wanted most of all was someone to talk to, and here he'd found a group of people expressing gratitude in a tranquil place. We can perhaps forgive him for thinking we were the kind of people who might be receptive to his attempt to connect.

We live in an amazing time. Being part of the Information Age gives us exposure to all kinds of wisdom and ancient teachings along with all the new. Yoga has been practiced for hundreds of years. Verses on gratitude can be found in the Bible. There is truth and power in these old ways, but let's make sure we're getting the most out of them. These ancient concepts should be more than just things you think to yourself or utter on autopilot. If we really want the benefits, we need to learn how to *live* them.

If you are grateful for something in your life, you have to find a way to put some of that grateful energy back into the world instead of holding onto it. That's the only way to keep it flowing. That's the only way gratitude can come back to you. If you have your antenna up while you perform your micro-gestures, you'll start to notice the flow and you'll start to better appreciate when some of it flows back your way.

HUMILITY IS AN EXPRESSION OF LOVE

There's something else you might find flowing your way as you practice your micro-gestures, and that's humility. Humility is kind of a strange concept in our world today, where we're encouraged to broadcast our accomplishments, share the minutia of our lives, and post about our happiest moments for all the world to see.

We don't live in the humblest of times, and we certainly don't typically elevate the humblest around us to celebrity status for all to admire. Yet most of us still believe that humility is a positive quality. We're turned off by arrogance, narcissism, and over-privilege when we see it in others, but I wonder how much time most of us spend cultivating humility in ourselves?

Think about humility in contrast to gratitude, which many people are all too willing to spend their time thinking or writing about in an attempt to cultivate it (though often in a far too passive way). And yet, I believe there's a relationship between gratitude and humility that hasn't gotten enough consideration. If we're truly grateful for what we've been given in life, we also have to humbly acknowledge that we aren't somehow inherently, cosmically, morally more deserving of it than someone else. I don't say this to belittle anyone's talent or diminish the hard work they've put in to get where they are—those things are meaningful and important, to be sure. What's also meaningful and important is the fact that there are people out there who work hard, who exercise their ample talents, but have fewer opportunities, or no opportunity at all, to feel loved, valued, or important for what they do and who they are.

If you haven't met such a person, then just trust me—I see them every day among my wildflowers. Most of us, if we're privileged enough to be reading a book like this, can't even imagine what that feels like, but we should take a moment to try—try to imagine just how far you would have gotten in your life if there had been no one on your side.

To make it more concrete, try to imagine what sort of chance someone who grew up in foster care and was passed around from family to family—some who were kind, others who really weren't—has to feel grounded and valued in this world. That person can certainly make something of him or herself—I know it because I've seen it—but it's a rough road from the start. It's easier to get in touch with our empathetic side when we have a greater understanding of where other people are coming from. For example, we recently had a volunteer named Annie who told us that she'd never been particularly interested in or sympathetic toward the problem of homelessness. But she worked with children, and when she discovered how many people on Skid Row had formerly been foster kids—more than half of foster children will end up on the streets within six months of aging out of the system—she suddenly saw things differently. She realized that she would have empathized with these same people when they were children—just a few years, or even months, earlier—so why should that feeling go away just because someone turns eighteen?

Often what most helps us to find more humility is a simple shift in perspective, and serving others invariably does that. It shifts our perspective from ourselves to others, from our own circumstances, which are so familiar to us, to the circumstances in which others live, which can be completely unfamiliar. This shift opens up space for more love, and it's something we could all use more practice at. Some mornings I wake up feeling tired and overwhelmed, and I want nothing more than a comforting cup of coffee to perk me up. If I get to my local coffee shop and there's a long line or an indecisive customer ahead of me, or the barista is inattentive, I can get impatient and annoyed. But when I get to work, my perspective invariably changes. When I'm reminded of all the many difficulties my street family contends with on a daily basis, the idea that what has upset me is nothing more than a delayed cup of coffee suddenly feels like a tremendous luxury.

WHY I GIVE A F♥CK . . .

"I was drinking and doing drugs when I was fourteen. Then I was on the street selling drugs. I got saved from a lot of situations in life that I feel like I shouldn't have been saved from—like I would be with friends and they'd get locked up but I wouldn't. It made me think, 'There's a reason why I was put here and I have to figure out what it is.' I've never really liked talking to people that much, but I like serving people. I know I'm supposed to be doing this because it's something I feel good doing."

EMILY
food recovery and zero waste manager, age 28

It's a gift that my work allows me this kind of perspective shift on a regular basis. But it's also not an accident. I actively put myself in positions where I can be of use, where I can be of service, and I try to remain open to the gifts that flow from these experiences. That's why the lessons come to me even when I'm not looking for them. And it can be the same for you. I always think of the Bible story of Jesus washing the feet of his disciples. It was something that Jesus didn't have to do. No one made him. No one suggested it would be a nice thing for him to do. He volunteered to do it. He chose to put himself in a space where he could practice his humility and his empathy, regardless of whether the people whose feet he washed "deserved" it. Because parsing what someone else deserved wasn't the point. The washing of the feet was the point. Humbling oneself to love and serve others was the one and only point.

EVERYONE NEEDS TO BE SEEN

Almost without exception, we underestimate one of the greatest gifts we have to give. It's something that every one of us has to offer. It doesn't matter if we're rich or poor, outgoing or introverted, in a good place in our lives or working things through, we all have this powerful thing to offer to strangers and loved ones alike: the power of our attention.

When you deal regularly with displaced people like I do, it becomes obvious pretty quickly how important it is to be seen. That's because people who live on the streets are regularly ignored and walked right past as if they don't exist. Even if you don't have money to spare for someone on the street who is asking for it, you can still say hello. You can still acknowledge the person's existence. I've known many displaced people who will stand outside a store and hold the door open for customers as they come and go. Sure, they might be hoping for your change, but I've learned that many of them do it just as much to be noticed. They are hoping someone will break up the monotony of their day by offering a smile and maybe a little conversation.

Of course, it's not just displaced people that this happens to. In our society, there are lots of people who are looked past on a regular basis, like the poor, the elderly, even children. Not long ago, LOM opened a bodega to bring fresh food to a neighborhood in Los Angeles where affordable, healthy food is hard to come by. We get a lot of families coming through, sometimes just to hang out because it's a welcoming and safe space. You can tell the difference right away between the children who are used to being seen and the ones who have learned to be detached and unobtrusive as they follow along behind their parents. We make a point of greeting every person who comes through the door, children included, whom we greet separately from their parents. We learn their names and use them when they come back. It's a simple gesture, so easy to do, but you'd be amazed how quickly most children will brighten up just because they've been spoken to directly.

The truth is that all of us want to be seen, no matter how old we are or what our experience has been. It frustrates me how often I see people withhold their attention when it could be given so easily. By "attention" I simply mean noticing someone, acknowledging someone, making eye contact and showing the person that you see him or her. It's not hard to do, and yet so many of us choose not to do it. Like in line at the grocery checkout, when I see someone texting with one hand and handing their credit card to the clerk with the other, never even looking up. Or when I see a couple out to dinner and one of them is on the phone while the other just sits and waits. Why do we do these things? How do we think people feel when they're standing right in front of us and we can't even bother to look at them? Is that how we want people to treat us?

It's not a loving way to be. It's also a misuse of our attention, which really is more powerful than we give it credit for. There's a man who hangs out near the bodega who is often so inebriated that he has difficultly standing up. When we first opened the store, we would find him slumped over nearby on a regular basis. Most people just walk right past him, but my colleagues and I have gotten into the habit of saying hello, talking to him, and offering him something to drink or eat. After a while, he started coming into the store on his own when he needed something to help him sober up. And then he started coming in sober more and more often. I think it's because he now has somewhere to go where he'll be seen and welcomed, and that alone gave him reason to want to be sober. He's not the only one. We made a friend named Scotty on Skid Row who said to us one day, "You bring me sobriety." All we do is offer him a little food and attention on a regular basis, and that's the effect it has had on him.

JOY IS CONTAGIOUS

In the second chapter of this book, I stressed the importance of understanding your privilege, and for a good reason. There's nothing wrong with having advantages, but there is something wrong with hoarding them. Our spirits suffer when we do because we cut off the flow of energy, the give and take that's needed for love to be a living thing in our lives. One of the ways in which we suffer when we hoard our gifts is that we close ourselves off to feelings of gratitude, humility, and also pure joy.

The amazing thing about joy is that it too can be found anywhere, and when you find it, it can be contagious. A couple of years ago, LOM did a back-to-school event at an elementary school in Watts, which has been identified by the Partnership for Los Angeles Schools as one of the "highest-need schools in the city."[5] We provided the kids with backpacks and other supplies they needed for school, but we wanted to go beyond that. Because we had been told that many of the children there had experienced a lot of stress, even trauma, during their short lives, we wanted to provide them with a chance to set that aside for the day and just have a good time. We brought in massage therapists and hairdressers. We offered yoga classes, dance classes, and face painting. Therapists who specialized in treating PTSD came to help out. It was amazing to watch how many of the kids, who were shy and withdrawn at first, opened themselves up to the experience.

There was one little five-year-old boy who was determined to try every single activity we offered, going from station to station to learn to dance and get his hair cut. When he got to the massage station, he was too small to fit in the chair. But that didn't stop him. He climbed up on that chair and waited for his massage. He slipped off, but then he climbed right back up. He slipped off again, but he wouldn't give up. Each time he would climb right back up as if it were just part of the experience. Finally he figured out how to hang on long enough for the therapist to gently knead his back, and he came away with the biggest smile on his face.

It was a lesson I'll never forget. There may be things in our lives that we can't control, and no one understands that better than a child, who has little control over his or her situation. Still, almost without exception, those kids were able to put their troubles aside and simply enjoy what they were being given at that moment. And their joy was contagious. The volunteers who came out to work that event still talk about it as one of the most memorable and inspiring days they've ever had.

I believe we can all have more joy in our lives if we just make a point of inviting it in. Even small moments can have a lasting impact. I can still picture the middle-aged man I met on Skid Row who was so thankful for the $10 gift card I gave him to get a sandwich at Subway—his favorite restaurant—that he literally went skipping off down the street to use it. A grown man, skipping! For something that cost me just $10. You better believe that I had a smile on my face for the rest of the day. It's worth asking ourselves on a regular basis:

When was the last time we got to witness joy like that? When was the last time we got to experience joy like that?

If it's not something that happens very often, or if you can't even remember the last time that it did, perhaps it's time to make more of an effort. You can use micro-gestures for this. You can use your gifts. You can check in more often with the ones you love. The point is that you have the power to create that kind of joy in the world. Don't you wonder what it would feel like if you made use of that power every day?

And when we do make use of that power, when we experience moments that touch us and others, we can take notice and build on them. We can ask ourselves why and then apply: What about my gift made this man so happy that he was moved to start skipping down the street? And what could I do for more people in my life that would make them feel like that? What would it mean to me if I did?

The more you do this, the easier it will become. In the next chapter, we'll talk about how powerful it can be to turn Love Without Reason into a regular habit.

♥ HEARTWORK ♥

Ask yourself why and then apply:

When was the last time you helped someone feel truly joyful? What happened? What did you do that made the person feel that way?

How did joy come back to you when you did that for someone else? Take note of how it made you feel and any lessons you learned from the experience.

How could you create that kind of moment more often in your life? Could you help more people in more situations to feel joyful?

If you were able to create more joyful moments, what would that mean to you?

Now that you've read about some of the lessons I've received from my wildflowers on Skid Row, ask yourself: *What spiritual lessons have I learned from my acts of service?*

6

LOVE IS A DISCIPLINE . . . AND A STEEPING

"Love is or it ain't. Thin love ain't love at all."

TONI MORRISON, *Beloved*[1]

We must always remember that this is about love after all. Love Without Reason is our purpose here, so it's important to ask ourselves: What is love anyway?

Love is something that practically everyone talks about. More stories, songs, and poems have been written about it than probably any other subject on the planet. People seem to think they know what it is, and yet their definitions can be all over the map. Love hurts. Love is blind. Love is noble. Love is cruel. Love is never having to say you're sorry. God is love.

When talking about romantic love, people often describe it as something you find. They say it's something you have to wait for or search for, something you long for until the right person comes along and sweeps you off your feet. You get shot by Cupid's arrow. You get struck by a bolt of lightning. And then you fall . . . fall in love. (Why do we have so many violent images of love?)

If the loving relationships in people's lives have been difficult—particularly the ones they experienced when they were young—they might think of love as a burden, a trial, maybe even as something that's for other people, but not for them. Others may think of love as something they reserve only for those closest to them—their partner, their children, their lifelong friend. Because love can be difficult, they think they need to conserve their energy by not spreading their love around.

So what has love meant to you? I believe we all need to spend some time thinking about this question. To answer, most people will draw on their past experiences of love, whether good, bad, or a little of both. This makes sense because love is personal. But there can be a problem with using only our own experiences to define love, which is that love existed long before any of us were around. When we attach love's meaning to our own experiences and only those experiences, we have to wonder if we're limiting its possibilities.

To gain even more perspective, we should ask ourselves not only what love means to us, but also what we *want* it to mean. Then we can compare whether what we want matches the role love has played in our lives so far. For example, if you're someone who instinctively says that love makes you vulnerable—maybe even too vulnerable—or causes pain, ask yourself whether that's the space you want love to hold in your life. Or would you rather it mean something else?

Even though love is a subject we're all familiar with, many (if not most) of us may need a new way of thinking about it. I don't believe that love is something you have to search for. I don't think it's something you just stumble across one day if you're lucky. No, I believe that love simply exists all around us, all the time. This means that every one of us has the capacity to call it forward whenever we want it. We can bring love into every experience we have if we choose to. If you think about it, this is really a tremendous power that each of us holds—if we can only learn how to wield it. Maybe it's time to stop being passive about the way love shows up in our lives. Maybe it's time to take love into our own hands.

❤ HEARTWORK ❤

Ask yourself: *What has love meant to me in my life?*

Some people will be able to answer this question right away, but for others it may be difficult. If you need a little help, start by thinking about the people who come to mind when you think about love. Write down their names. Then look at each name one by one and write down the primary ways that person makes you feel (beyond the feeling of love, of course). For some people, positive words may spring to mind, like "supported," "cherished," or "protected." For others, more complicated words may come, like "vulnerable," "manipulated," or "neglected." Don't over-think it: just write down what comes up for you.

Next, ask yourself: *What do I want love to mean going forward?*

It's important that we remind ourselves that just because something has been one way in the past doesn't mean it has to continue to be that way in the future. Maybe there's something about how love has shown up in your life that you would like to be different in the future. Don't worry about how you're going to make that happen just yet. Instead, think about what you'd like to experience when you experience love, and allow yourself to dream a little. What would be your ideal?

Again, this question may be tough for some people to answer. If you find yourself stuck, try flipping the question on its head and ask yourself what you *don't* want love to mean. Write down everything you can think of. Then look back at what you wrote and ask yourself: *What would be the opposite of these things I don't want?*

TAKING LOVE INTO OUR OWN HANDS

I didn't always think of love this way. When I was growing up, love was confusing. I understood that parents are supposed to love their children, but like many children of an abusive parent, I didn't know how to reconcile that idea with the way my birth mom treated me. And not just me, but the way she treated everyone. My conception of love was affected by my experiences, like the time I watched my birth mom stab my dad with a knife just because she was angry at him. Another time she tried to light him on fire. What did her angry, unstable, and sometimes violent energy have to do with love? My young mind wasn't yet capable of figuring out the answer.

Not surprisingly, I eventually became angry, unstable, and sometimes violent too. But the things that set me off were often different than what inflamed my birth mom. People who know me now are often surprised to learn that I got into a lot of fights growing up, but I didn't do it because I wanted to hurt people. I did it because I wanted to defend them and I didn't know a better way. I remember once, when I was a teenager, coming across a boy who was beating up a disabled girl who lived in our neighborhood. I saw her there, huddled on the ground with her arms over her head, trying to shield herself but unable to fight back. I recognized that position because I'd been in the same one before with my birth mom standing over me. I lost it. I ran straight at that boy and let loose on him.

It was pure instinct. That girl's helplessness felt so familiar. Using violence to gain power in a situation felt familiar too. But just because something is familiar doesn't make it right. And just because something is familiar doesn't mean it has to stay that way.

We all have a tendency to accept our own experiences as "that's just the way things are" or "that's the way the world works," without asking a lot of questions. I was not loved well in a lot of situations growing up. I had to learn to accept that and stop fighting against it because none of us can go backward. We can't change how things were, no matter how much we may want to. But accepting the past does not have to be the end of our story. We can also decide not to let how things were determine how things will be going forward. I was not loved well in a lot of situations growing up, but that didn't stop me from wanting to be. And I realized that if I wanted things to be different, I had to rewrite the definition of love that I'd grown up with.

When defining what we want love to mean in our lives, it can be easier to start by deciding what we *don't* want it to be. I didn't want love to equal abuse. I didn't want love to be about yelling or disrespecting people. I didn't want love to be about holding grudges or withholding affection. A new definition starts with a decision. It starts with each of us saying to ourselves: *I don't want love to be like this anymore. I want it to be something else—something better.*

Deciding what I didn't want love to be created room for new possibilities. I was lucky in that my birth mom was not the only example of love that I could draw from. I had my dad, who was not my birth father but who had chosen to love me nonetheless. I had my best friend Jamila, who'd been by my side since we were five. I had the people I was reading about in books when I needed to escape. Most of all, I had my grandmother, who was the purest example of love I'll ever know. The more I looked, the more I realized that there were examples of love all around me and that I could choose the version that felt best to me.

Eventually, when I was old enough to understand better, I realized that what I was receiving from my birth mom wasn't love at all. It was something else, and I wanted something more. I wanted love to be a positive force in my life, for my own sake as well as the sake of those around me.

I believe we're all capable of making these sorts of decisions about love. It may not be easy, but you don't have to do it all at once. You can start by deciding what you don't want. Then you can begin to imagine what could be instead. Once you've done that, you can work toward that new definition each and every day. That's the discipline of love. It may not be easy, but it's definitely worth it.

❤ HEARTWORK ❤

Look back at your answers to these two questions in the previous Heartwork exercise: *What has love meant to me in my life?* and *What do I want love to mean going forward?* Compare your answers to these two questions.

If there's a difference between the two, spend some time thinking about ways in which you might move your current definition of love a little closer to the definition of love that you're hoping for. For example, if the word "distant" came to mind as something you'd like to change, then look at your relationships and think about what you could do to be less distant to the people you love. Could you put down your phone more often when your children talk to you? Could you call your friends instead of waiting for them to call you? Could you say "I love you" more often to your spouse?

You don't have to come up with grand gestures. Think about which actions, big or small, would help others feel love as you would like it to be defined. Then pick one gesture and try it out this week. Put down your phone every time someone you love is talking to you, for example, and see what happens.

I've said before that I believe we will start getting what we want out of life when we learn how to give it, so this is not only a way to start being the kind of loving person you want to be, but also to start showing others how you want to be loved. Once you've tried one gesture and gotten used to it, try another, and another. In this way, we can intentionally shift our definition of love, bit by bit, to a new and more empowering place.

LOVE AS A DISCIPLINE

Maybe it's because love is this ever-present topic in stories and songs that it gets taken for granted far too often in real life. But love doesn't just happen. In fact, the state of the world can easily make you unloving if you don't actively, continually counteract it with something. Like I said before, I believe that love exists all around us. I believe that it's there, ready for us to call on and to cultivate at any time, but we have to take action to bring it forward. And we have to keep taking action if we want it to stick around. We have to change our mindset from being passive about love to being intentionally loving every day, or at least as often as we can.

Think of love the way you might think about sunlight. On some days the sun shines brightly, while on others it's obscured behind the clouds. Sometimes we're inspired to get outside and bask in the sun. Other times, we stay inside, draw the shades, and hide ourselves away. Either way, the light is there. It exists whether we can see it or not. It exists whether we embrace it or shut it out. It exists whether we make use of it or not. Its energy permeates our world every day no matter who we are, and it never asks whether some of us are more entitled to or deserving of it than anyone else.

The energy of love is the same. It's already there for us. It *is* us. It always has been. And it's waiting for us to make use of it. People put so much emphasis on love as a thing, but just like gratitude, love, I believe, is a verb. Love is in the doing, in the action, in the encounters we have with another human being. The discipline of love comes when you take those actions consistently and with intention. That discipline is what will counteract everything the world can do to you. That's what I realized when I put the contorted lessons my birth mom had taught me about love behind me.

This is why it's so important to consciously create our own definition of love. Because unless you want to leave it up to an often unkind world to set the stage for love in your life, you can't be passive about it. You can't treat it as something that might hit you one day when you're least expecting it, like Cupid's arrow or a bolt of lightning. Real love is intentional, not accidental. Deep love is a practice that you cultivate over time. If you want love (as the noun) to be in your life every day, then you have to be intentionally loving (as the verb) every day.

That's what it means to be disciplined about love. We tend to willingly put effort into the things we value in life. If we want a certain type of career, we might go to school to study the subject. Or we work at it, maybe rising through the ranks in a company or working for someone who is thriving in the field. If we want to be better parents, we might read books or blogs, listen to experts, and consult those close to us whose parenting skills we admire. If we want to take up martial arts, we're almost surely going to enroll in classes, practice at home, maybe even compete in tournaments. Why do we think love should be any different than anything else we want to be good at? If we want to love well, then why wouldn't we put in the effort? I'm not saying it's easy, but show me what good things in life are.

BRING LOVE INTO EVERY ENCOUNTER THAT YOU CAN

So how do you become more disciplined about love? I like to think it's like learning how to swim, ride a bike, or meditate. You begin simply by trying. And then you try again. And again. And when you fail or fall, you pick yourself up and do it again. That's the way we learn how to do anything in life. That's the way we get better at anything. It's often hard at first, but you chip away at it. And if you do that, then at some point you'll find it's not so hard anymore. Just like with anything that you practice, love gets easier. And if you treat it as a discipline, as something you practice every day, then you can become a master of it.

MASTERING LOVE: AN EVOLUTION

One micro-gesture →
   several micro-gestures→
      a daily practice of micro-gestures→
         a daily practice of love

The practice of love becomes a habit→
    practiced habits become innate →
      love becomes who you are

Kicking off this kind of evolution is really what micro-gestures are meant for. A micro-gesture is a small, simple, intentional act of love—a first step toward mastery. You start by trying one. And then you do another. Then you do them more and more often, thereby turning micro-gestures into a regular practice. Pretty soon you'll become more comfortable and more familiar with the energy of giving and caring, sharing and loving, because the practice becomes a habit. Practiced disciplines become habits and practiced habits become innate. This is the road to mastery.

You probably have some sense of what it means to master a martial art or a musical instrument, but what does it mean to master love? The purpose behind being disciplined about love is for loving acts to become so common in your life, such second-nature to you, that you no longer need to practice. If you do it enough, then you learn to identify with being loving. It becomes as natural to you as eating or breathing. It becomes not just something you do, but who you are. You want to get to the point where when your actions are not born out of love, you don't feel like you're being yourself because love is such an integral part of who you are. Being unloving is what will feel unnatural. This is mastery.

What this looks like in everyday practice is you bringing love into every single encounter that you have throughout the day. That's what our discipline is building toward. As you practice micro-gestures more and more often, you'll find that the practice starts to expand into more and more parts of your day and that you're acting out of love toward more people in more contexts. And more and more and more, until you become a walking, talking expression of love.

Of course, we may never reach that ultimate point, but that's okay. We can still aim for that ideal. It's a big, grand ideal to be sure, but it's important to set our sights high. Otherwise, we can end up treating love as a pastime, rather than a discipline, because we're not putting in consistent effort. We have all experienced this during encounters with different people in our lives. Often you'll recognize it by the sense of betrayal or hypocrisy you feel when someone is only bringing the love part time.

For example, not long ago I was invited to participate in a MindBodyGreen conference that brought together a diverse group of experts to talk about the subject of wellness in different aspects of life—mental, physical, emotional, spiritual, and even environmental. During a lunch break, speakers and audience members alike sat together at communal tables to eat. My colleague Venus was sitting there with an empty chair next to her when a woman sat down. It turned out to be one of the speakers, someone who is pretty well known for her talks on the subjects of love and community.

Venus didn't recognize the woman, but she turned to say hello and introduce herself all the same, just to be polite. But the woman immediately cut her off. "I can't talk to you right now," she said without apology. "I don't like talking in the morning."

I hadn't heard what the woman said, but I could tell by the look on Venus's face that she was more than a little stunned by it. Still, she turned away and gave the woman her space. Not even five minutes later, the woman struck up a very loud, very animated conversation with the man sitting on the other side of her—a doctor who was one of the better-known speakers at the conference. I guess she woke up all of sudden and regained her capacity to speak—but she didn't seem to care about the fact that she'd just stacked one rude gesture on top of another toward my friend.

At the end of this book, I've included a menu of micro-gestures to help you think broadly and creatively about the ways in which you can give a f♥ck about others. When you read through them, you'll notice that a significant number revolve around helping others feel welcome and accepted. That's because we all want to feel this way, but the world we live in can make it difficult. Obviously, the woman who brushed off Venus didn't share my feelings about the value of this kind of gesture.

An important thing to remember is that attempting to bring love into a simple encounter like this one isn't just about making the other person feel good. It's also about us. We will never know how many opportunities we're missing by writing people off without giving them a chance. The woman who sat next to Venus was obviously caught up in the idea that she needed to network with "important" people, like the well-known doctor she eventually saw fit to talk to. But in the process, she was missing a golden opportunity to connect with someone who, I happen to know, is a totally unique and incredible person, someone who has a great depth of experience in the subjects of love and community, which were topics this woman spoke about professionally. If she hadn't been so oblivious, she could have experienced that for herself.

We're all going to have our lesser moments in life, times when we fall short of the ideal or miss opportunities. That's just part of being human, and I'm not suggesting that we beat ourselves up about it. But we can admit when we stumble. If it had been me, and I was sitting in my hotel room the next morning, checking in with myself before starting my day, I would have spent some time thinking about the encounter and why it had unfolded the way it did. If I knew how to get in touch with her, I would have contacted the person to whom I'd been so dismissive and apologized. Whether or not that was possible, I would have thought about what I could do differently the next time to be more open and caring. Perhaps if the speaker had taken a moment to check in with herself and her emotions before going into the lunchroom (like we talked about in chapter 4 regarding how energy exchange works), she would have acted differently. Or, if she had checked in with herself and realized that she was too depleted to be good company, she could have found a space to be by herself and recharge. After all, we were all staying in the hotel where the conference was being held, so presumably she had a room right upstairs where she could have avoided talking to people if it was that important to her.

The point is that we always have options. We can always choose to be more caring, more generous, more loving in every moment we encounter. Being aware of that is the first step. The second is to challenge ourselves to make more loving choices more often in our lives. If we acknowledge that every encounter is an opportunity, then we next need to ask ourselves: How well are we taking advantage of the opportunities we're given every day?

LOVE IN OUR OWN HOUSEHOLDS

For most of us, the people we encounter most often are the people we share a home with, which is why home is where you'll find some of the greatest opportunities to build more love in your life. And many of us need to examine whether we're making the most out of the opportunities we're given.

Now, a lot of people like to say that love starts at home, but that can be a problematic idea. Love doesn't start at home for everyone. It certainly didn't start there for me, and maybe it didn't start there for you either. Or maybe it did, but it was a murky or complicated feeling, one where love got all tied up with other things like power struggles, manipulation, or something else. Maybe you felt love growing up, but only if you did what you were told or excelled in school. If not, then love might have been withheld from you.

Maybe you found a purer, more empowering form of love somewhere else, like at your grandparents' home, in your first romantic relationship, or in the presence of your best friend. Or maybe you felt loved growing up, but in adulthood you haven't been able to find a loving relationship with a partner that will last. Or maybe you've had love in the past, but there's not much of it at home right now. You might even be one of those people who has given a lot to the world but hasn't always been as generous with what you offered to those closest to you. The truth is that none of us has a perfect love story, but that doesn't mean we are somehow undeserving. And it certainly doesn't mean we are powerless to change how love is showing up in our household right now.

What we can do is simply let love start where it starts. That may be different for each of us—at home for some, somewhere else for others—and that's fine. There's no reason why our love stories should all be the same. What's important is that we don't let the limits of our past experiences define us and we don't use the absence of love in our past as an excuse not to bring it into our present. Love is love, so start from wherever you have found love in your life, no matter where that was, and then build from there.

We can begin to build more love by being mindful and honest with ourselves about how we show love to those closest to us. Most of us like to define ourselves as loving, caring people, especially when it comes to family, but if that's how we want to think of ourselves, then we have to challenge ourselves by asking how and when:

How was I loving when I was short-tempered with my children this morning? Well, you probably weren't. I'm sure you love your children, but that's not the same as acting lovingly toward them in that moment. Or: When am I being loving if I spend most of my time by myself in front of the TV or closed off in my office? You can't be loving in isolation. Love only comes through in your interactions with people. It can be found in your encounters, which is why each one is an opportunity.

It's the discipline of love that allows us to take charge of how we want our love to come across. It's also what allows us to disrupt old patterns that aren't supporting our new definition of love. That's what happened with my siblings. We used to yell a lot when we talked to one another until I challenged myself to change that unloving dynamic. First, I decided I just wasn't going to talk to them that way anymore. Then, I brought that intention into every interaction we had with each other, one encounter at a time. It didn't take long for them to notice that when they yelled, I didn't yell back. That's when I let them know that it was my intention to speak more lovingly to them from then on. Eventually they stopped yelling too. It was a gradual change, but it has been a lasting one.

If sometimes—or even most of the time—our encounters with the ones we love aren't unfolding in a loving way, we can always challenge ourselves by asking why and then asking what we can do to change things. We can also set the intention to make the most out of as many of these opportunities as we can, both at home and when we're out in the world. Is that a lot to ask of ourselves? Of course it is, but perhaps not as much as you think.

♥ HEARTWORK ♥

Ask yourself: *How and when did I act lovingly today?*

and then . . .

If there were moments when I didn't act lovingly today, what happened? What role did I play in the encounter? What could I do differently next time?

EVERY ENCOUNTER? BUT ISN'T THAT EXHAUSTING?

I get a lot of questions from people about the "downsides" of love. They can't possibly be loving during *every* encounter in their lives, can they? It just sounds too draining. They'll end up exhausting themselves, and then where will they be? They'll have nothing left over to give to their families. They'll have nothing left over for themselves. I think some people even believe that it could kill them to love too much—at least that's the way it sounds when they talk about it.

It's a concept that I constantly have to push back on. Where did the idea that love is depleting come from anyway?

I think it can be traced back to what we believe about love, which is why I started this chapter by asking you to consider your definition of it. A lot of us think of love as this finite resource. It's like we're given a cupful of it at birth and that's all we get. And if that's all we get, we have to be careful not to waste it or spill it or use it up on the wrong person. Otherwise it will be gone, and we'll be left with nothing but an empty cup.

But that's not been my experience at all. I personally never look at my cup as drained—not anymore—because I believe that I can always fill my own cup. When you know you are your own source of love, then you don't worry about running out. Love comes from an infinite place, and as long as you're around, you always have the capacity to make love happen.

I think it's a misunderstanding to say that love drains you, because it's not love that does this. It's the world we live in and how it seems to place a lot of value on things that are about anything but love. It's people and how they have a tendency to treat others in ways that are not loving, or to call something love when it's really a means to manipulate, control, or hurt. But it's not love itself. In fact, I believe it's the absence of love in so many facets of our life that so often makes us feel exhausted, unhappy, and depleted.

There are two ideas that I hope people will consider in order to help them overcome the fear of loving too much. First, love has a way of finding a natural balance. When we withhold love from others, it tends to be withheld from us. Of course, the opposite is true too: the more loving we are, the more love we invite into our lives.

The second idea is this: becoming more focused on and disciplined about love makes life a lot simpler. And if we can simplify our lives, then we'll have more energy, not less, to spend on loving people, including ourselves.

Not sure you believe me? Think about all the mental energy people spend on trying to figure out the best way to handle a situation or approach a person. I've listened as people go through mental contortions trying to figure out the right thing to do. For me, the right thing to do is always the same, so I don't have to think about it. It's always going to be right to approach every person in every situation with love.

At one of my speeches recently, a woman stood up to ask me a question, and I could tell right away that she was exhausting herself by trying to think through all the possible implications of becoming a giver. She talked about this man in her neighborhood whom she often had the impulse to try to help, but she suspected he might be a drug addict and she didn't want to enable him. So she never approached him, never did anything for him, but she always wondered if she was doing the right thing. She wanted to know what I thought she should do.

My answer to her was "don't overthink it." Maybe he is a drug addict and maybe he isn't. Are you going to require a drug test from every person you're contemplating caring about? That sounds like a lot of work. And what if he is a drug addict? Does that mean he doesn't deserve any love or care? I mean, none of us is perfect, so what equation are we going to use to determine what level of imperfection merits what level of caring? Talk about exhausting. Especially when we can keep it simple: Everyone deserves love. There are no exceptions. Start there and suddenly there's a lot less to worry about.

For those who are concerned about how draining it could be to Love Without Reason, I wonder if they've considered how much energy they spend on not loving. How much effort does it take to withhold our love when our instinct is to offer it? How much time and effort do we spend on judging people, avoiding people, pushing people away, and finding reasons not to care about them? How draining is it to argue with people or fight with them? It takes work to love, but it takes work to guard our hearts too. So what's more worthy of our time and effort?

Besides, I believe it actually takes less effort to be loving than it does to be guarded and withholding because it's in our nature to love. We don't need to learn how to be good people. We're already good people. Some of us have just forgotten because we got a little lost along the way. We lost who we were as children, when we were so naturally excited to share and to give, when we loved so freely and fully. We lost our connection to that version of ourselves in everything the world has taught us as we grew into adults. But we can get that child back. We can get realigned with our true nature if we make the choice to and then put in the work.

ALLOW FOR MISTAKES

One of the things that can derail any kind of discipline is when we feel we've made a mistake. When we feel like we're failing, or something is just too difficult to maintain, we might have the instinct to give up. That's why it's important to remember that not only is every encounter an opportunity to practice love, but every encounter is also an opportunity to recover or renew our discipline if we've fallen short. And when we fall short, we can do what I suggested that speaker who was rude to my friend, Venus, should have done: we can examine and admit to our part in it.

Once we do that, however, it's also important to give ourselves a break. Perfection isn't required of us because perfection is impossible. When we take away the impulse to live up to impossible standards, it creates more room for self-correction and growth. It also helps to keep in mind that self-correction is something we can do at any time, whenever we catch ourselves. We can recognize after the fact that we messed up and tell ourselves that we would really like to do better next time.

Or we can finish an angry argument with someone, and then go back a day later, or a week later, or even years later and say to that person: "I'm sorry. That isn't how I wanted that to go."

Or we can catch ourselves mid-mistake and say: "I'm sorry. I'm yelling and I don't want to be. Let's take a breath."

Or even if we didn't mean it that way, but we can tell by someone's energy that they're getting upset by what we're saying or how we're saying it, we can stop ourselves and say: "I'm sorry. I'm speaking too loudly. I didn't mean to make it seem like I'm mad at you. I'm not. I'm just passionate about what I'm saying."

So many people have trouble admitting their mistakes and saying they're sorry, which I personally have trouble understanding. I find that it's so very liberating once you can get over that barrier. I'm not suggesting that you become one of those people who apologizes all the time—you should save the "I'm sorrys" for when they're deserved so that they have more resonance—but try to recognize that those two little words are easy to say and take none of your power away. So if you're one of those people who just finds it soooo difficult, then (like anything else you want to master) practice it:

I'm sorry.

I'm sorry.

I'm sorry.

I think you'll be surprised how those two little words, if said convincingly (it should go without saying that you have to mean it), can take so much of the air out of a difficult encounter. And if they don't, then don't worry about it. In all our encounters, in every situation, we only have to be responsible for doing our part. If we've tried our best to make a positive difference, if we've done everything we can to correct our behavior after we stumbled, then whatever happens next is out of our hands—so let it go.

We have a tendency to set ourselves up for failure by being so outcome-oriented, but it's the process that matters most. This is about developing the discipline of love and sticking to it as best we can. And then letting what happens happen.

We don't have to be afraid of messing up when it comes to love because built into love is the capacity for forgiving ourselves and others. Mess up, take from the experience what you can, correct what you're able to, and then move on to the next encounter—the next opportunity to be loving. There's nothing to fear here. What we should really be afraid of is being stagnant, of not learning or expanding, of not letting ourselves steep in these experiences so they can change us.

Love can be complicated and confusing. Love can sometimes feel cruel. Love can be difficult to get right. And all that can make us feel like we don't want to try. But it's in the trying that things get easier. It's in the doing that you'll find your bearings and eventually your power.

You don't need to sit in your room practicing or reading this book a bunch of times before you put yourself out there. You don't need to attend a bunch of spirituality classes and shed all your pain before you start your practice. You don't need to try to make yourself perfect. You're going to have some bad encounters, you're going to mess them up sometimes, and that's okay. You're more resilient than you think.

What it really comes down to is not waiting to feel better about yourself or the world before you risk your heart. You can't wait because it doesn't work that way. In fact, it's the other way around: you need to risk your heart in order to feel better about yourself and the world.

❤ HEARTWORK ❤
ANATOMY OF AN APOLOGY

Part of the discipline of love is knowing when and how to say you're sorry to someone you've hurt or wronged in some way. Begin by asking yourself: *How often do I apologize for my mistakes or for hurting someone either intentionally or unintentionally?*

If the answer is "not very often," then it's time to ask yourself why. Because none of us is perfect, apologies are an invaluable tool for supporting loving encounters. Being able to fearlessly

---

admit when we're wrong is also critical for our personal growth. Otherwise, we're sure to repeat our mistakes.

So if apologies don't come easy to you, ask yourself: *What's standing in my way?*

If you find them difficult because you just aren't sure how to do them well, consider the following components of a good apology:

1) **Authenticity:** There is nothing worse than a hollow apology. Take a moment (or more if needed) before apologizing to understand how your actions or words affected the other person so that you aren't just saying sorry, but actually feeling sorry for what happened. Apologies aren't supposed to be about giving up your power or even establishing who is right or who is wrong. They are about letting people know that you care about them and their feelings. So first, you have to care.

2) **Clarity:** When you do say "I'm sorry," don't stop there, and don't be vague or offhanded about it. Make it clear what you're apologizing for: "I'm sorry for [fill in the blank]."

3) **Acknowledgment:** Show the person that you understand how you hurt or negatively affected him or her: "I'm sorry I was late and didn't call. You must have been worried, and I can see now that it screwed up your plans."

4) **Listening:** Don't assume that that's the end. You have to allow the person to respond. If it's not already clear, encourage the person to tell you how your actions impacted him or her and what you can do to make things better.

One of the reasons people find it difficult to apologize is because they worry their apology won't be accepted. Remember that the next time someone apologizes to you, even if it's not done perfectly. You can still support the person and your mutual relationship by taking a moment to react well to the apology by 1) acknowledging it, 2) accepting it, and 3) honoring it.

LOVE IS A STEEPING . . . SO ENJOY THE PROCESS

I've said it before, but I think it's worth repeating at this point: LWR isn't just something you do for other people or for the world around you. It's also something you do for yourself.

Every day I think about how I can bring more love into more of my encounters with others. I may never reach the goal of making *every* encounter I'm part of a loving one, but I can try. Having that as my ideal has helped change my day-to-day perspective so that I actively look for more areas of my life in which to let the loving energy flow, bringing love to more people, in more places, during more moments in my day. You can do the same. You can let love infuse your entire life in time. Love Without Reason is about leading a fuller, richer, more loving life. It's a way of living in love. Of steeping yourself in it.

I'm talking about making a big shift here— in the way you view and treat others, and in the way you view and treat yourself—but also a gradual one. I used to own a café, and the gradualness always makes me think of brewing a cup of tea. Growing in love is a kind of steeping. When you make tea, the longer you keep the leaves in the water, the more infused the water gets. The color gets darker, the flavor gets stronger and more complex. Herbal tea especially gets better the longer you let the leaves steep.

It's in this same way that our relationship with love can deepen and strengthen. There's no need to rush the process. In fact, you shouldn't rush it. You should take your time and savor it. When you perform even one loving gesture, one micro-gesture, you're exercising your heart muscle. Take a moment afterward to notice how that feels. Notice how it sits in your body. Pay attention to how it registers in your mind. Our experiences stay with us. They are what change us, so pay attention to what brings about the change.

And then create more of the kind of moments you want to define your life. Because one act of love is never going to be enough. Like one of my

WHY I GIVE A F♥CK . . .

"You can't be a doctor without having some sort of heart for people, without wanting to help. It's natural for me. It's my personality to want to do something better than worry about myself. It makes me feel like I accomplished something when I help someone. It makes me feel like the time I was given in this world, I didn't waste it—at least not today. A lot of people get caught up in me me me, but it's no burden to be loving. You can walk away from every day feeling good about what you've done."

JAMES
surgeon, age 53

all-time favorite writers, Toni Morrison, wrote in the novel *Beloved*: "Thin love ain't love at all." It's like weak tea—what's the point? You've got to let it steep, deepen, and infuse the whole of your being. We can create big change this way—one moment at a time, layered one on top of each other. Pretty soon you'll see that love isn't a burden at all. It isn't something that will exhaust you or make you weak. When you steep in love long enough, then you can master it. And when you master love, you will rise in it. It becomes the source from which you can draw power and inspiration. It becomes the thing that fortifies you when times get tough. It becomes your regular source of joy.

7

WHEN LOVE IS LABOR

"Love takes off the masks that we fear we cannot live without and know we cannot live within. I use the word 'love' here not merely in the personal sense but as a state of being, or a state of grace—not in the infantile American sense of being made happy but in the tough and universal sense of quest and daring and growth."

JAMES BALDWIN, *The Fire Next Time*[1]

I believe that love is limitless, but even if you embrace that idea, it doesn't mean that it's easy to love people. Somewhere along the way, we all have probably had a moment when we wish we hadn't tried—because the people we love can hurt us sometimes. When the inevitable happens, what can we do? If we want to stay disciplined about love, then we need to know how to handle it when loving is difficult.

When my grandfather was dying, he forbade everyone in the family from visiting him in the hospital. Hospitals aren't very nice places to visit in the first place, plus he was *really* grumpy about it, so most of my family went along with his demand. But I couldn't do it. I knew I would regret it if I didn't say goodbye. Besides, I didn't really believe that he wanted to die alone. I think he was just afraid. I think he didn't want the people he loved to see him in a weakened state, because he didn't want us to remember him that way. But that didn't mean it would be okay to let him go without at least trying to show him how loved he was. And it didn't mean that it would be okay for me to turn away from an important experience just because he was making it difficult.

So I called my best friend, Jamila, who had known my grandfather her whole life too, and asked her if she would come with me for support. The two of us picked up some pizza and showed up at his room. We didn't ask; we just went.

My grandfather didn't make it easy on us. He was gruff at first, wanting to know what we were doing there, asking why I hadn't done what he'd asked. I kept telling him that I couldn't help it: I loved him too much to stay away. He didn't fight me forever. After a while he let it go, and we ended up—believe it or not—actually having fun. I was reminded of all the pizza parties we'd had when I was young and my grandfather would take Jamila and me out to eat. We talked and we laughed, and I got a chance to tell him how much it had meant to me to have him in my life. He died not long after, and I'll never be sorry that I got to be with him in his last moments, even if those moments weren't always comfortable for either of us.

People can be confusing. And frustrating. And just plain maddening at times. When you set out to master something, as we're intending to do with love, it never comes without its setbacks or trying times. This is one of the big reasons why it's so helpful to treat love as a discipline. When love becomes something that you're dedicated to practicing every day, then that setback you're having, that difficult encounter, becomes just one moment in a long chain of loving moments. And it's a moment where you've been before. It's the moment when you fell before you got back on your bike. It's the competition you lost before you earned your black belt. It's the relationship that ended before you found your true partner. It's just one moment in a long journey, and sometimes when love hurts the most, that's when you know it's the most worth it.

ABUSE ISN'T LOVE

Before we get too far into this topic, I want to make sure I'm very clear about something important: I'm not suggesting that anyone endure abuse for the sake of love. While I believe in extending my heart even when someone isn't always careful with it, that doesn't mean I will allow anyone to beat it up over and over again. Not anymore. I learned that lesson long ago. Loving someone should never require you to put your self-love on the back burner.

Nor am I suggesting that you become a pushover. Quite the opposite: I'm suggesting you make love a source of your power, not a reason to compromise your value.

This was a lesson I learned because of my birth mom. When I was old enough, I chose to no longer have a relationship with her, and that decision has stuck to this day. I don't believe it was an unloving one either. In fact, I believe I have a greater capacity for love because of it. My relationship with her forced me to define for myself what I wanted love to be. Once that definition was clear, I was able to insist on it being part of all my relationships. If it couldn't be, that meant I had to let the relationship go.

It's important to remember that this might be another area of life that makes us uncomfortable because we know we've made some mistakes. We may have allowed people in the past, or present, to treat us poorly without sticking up for ourselves. We may have even stayed in abusive situations after our attempts at bringing more love into the relationship failed. We can forgive ourselves for that. After all, it takes some knowledge and life experience to figure out where the lines should be drawn and what we want love to mean. No matter what has happened in the past, you always have the right to change the dynamic of a relationship.

If someone is simply difficult, I do believe in giving that person a chance to meet me in a more loving place. But there have to be limits. Whatever makes you feel like you're compromising your self-love, your own value, is a hard and fast limit for me. But it isn't a limit on love. It's a limit on the relationship, a limit on whether that person can be part of your life. You can go ahead and love the person from afar if you want to. In fact, setting a healthy boundary can, in itself, be an act of caring and love.

TRY TO ACCEPT PAIN FOR WHAT IT IS

The people we love can be a source of pain. That's a reality we cannot avoid, so it's really a misuse of energy to try to deny it or escape it by putting up walls or keeping people at a distance. After all, feeling isolated and alone can be a great source of pain too, so avoiding people isn't really the answer. Closing off our hearts isn't the answer either. Because pain is an inevitable part of life, it's something we have to learn to deal with. I know what you're probably thinking—easier said than done—but we can at least make things a little simpler for ourselves by accepting the reality instead of fighting against it.

The best thing we can do for ourselves, and for others, is to work to keep our pain right-sized. We can try to accept it as an inevitable part of life without letting it take up more area in our lives than it needs to. Because the people we love can cause us pain, there's a misconception that often happens. Sometimes pain becomes attached to people's definition of love, i.e., "I love this person, and this person hurt me, so love must equal hurt." But pain isn't love. Pain is pain.

In the last chapter, we talked about having a clear conception of what love means to us and what it doesn't, or shouldn't. In the same way, we need to get clear about pain. That's because it's something that has a tremendous effect on us. We react to pain in ways that are often instinctual, and we may structure our lives or our behaviors in ways that we think will help us avoid it. So often we do this without even giving the subject much thought.

So what is pain? It can be a lot of things, but the most important thing that it is (at least for our purposes here) is a signal. It's a call for attention. We're more likely to understand this and honor it when the pain is in our body. If you feel a twinge in your back, you know that you may have injured yourself or pushed yourself too far and some extra care and attention is needed. A pain or soreness in the back of your throat can be a sign that a cold is coming on and you need to take it easy, feed yourself nourishing food, and get some extra rest.

So what does it mean when, say, someone waves off our gesture of caring and we feel the sting of rejection? It means the same as it would if we were feeling a sting in our body somewhere, maybe from a bee or prickly rose bush: it's a signal that there's something there that we need to pay attention to and to heal.

But, didn't I start off this chapter by talking about *other people* and how *they* can be so incredibly difficult? Yes, I did. So why am I now talking about you? Why am I talking about *your* pain and not *their* behavior?

Because when love feels like labor, it's not really about the other person. It's about you. You're the one who's feeling that way, and that feeling is what needs to be addressed. We can't control anyone else's behavior toward us, but we can control how we deal with it. That's how we empower ourselves in difficult situations. We can empower ourselves by choosing to respond to that difficult situation or difficult person with love—for the other person and for ourselves.

And when I talk about pain, I'm talking about it broadly. I'm talking about any of the unhappy or uncomfortable or negative feelings that may come up during an encounter with someone. Pain can come through as feelings of anger, fear, shame, rejection, disgust, or so many other things. Pain can show up in a million different ways, but the exact nature of the feeling isn't what matters most here. What matters is your ability to recognize it for what it is: a sign that something needs to be addressed because it's keeping you from feeling and expressing love.

That's the first step in addressing love's labor. The next step is to choose how you want to relate to your pain going forward.

CHOOSE WHERE YOU WANT TO SIT

There are three important things about pain that we all could benefit from understanding before we move forward:

1) Pain is inevitable.

2) Pain is a signal that healing needs to happen.

3) Pain is a barrier to love.

First, pain is inevitable, so why put energy toward fighting it or running from it? That energy could be better spent on something else, couldn't it? Second, if pain is a clue that we need to be healed in some way, then there is something we can do about it. It may be inevitable that we feel pain, but that doesn't mean our pain controls us.

Third, if pain is a barrier to love, then isn't that all the motivation we need to work toward healing it? After all, isn't love something we all want more of in our lives? And isn't pain something we want to, if not avoid, at least minimize or move on from as quickly as possible?

You'd think so, but that isn't the way things play out a lot of the time. Sometimes we can get really attached to our pain. We may even use it to define who we are. It's certainly where a lot of people place their focus, which you might notice when you ask them the simple question of how they're doing. If you don't get a generic "I'm fine" type answer, then what you'll hear most is people talking about what's wrong in their lives—that they're feeling sick or stressed out or in the midst of some unwanted circumstance. What you don't often get is someone saying, "You know what? I'm really glad you asked me that because I'm having a great day today and I'm happy to be here with you!"

We place a lot of emphasis on the negative, and it's not even all our fault. In psychology they call it the "negativity bias," and it means that the human brain is hardwired to place greater emphasis on negative rather than positive information.[2] It's the reason why a compliment may not stick in our heads the same way that an insult does, or why we feel compelled to write a Yelp review about the one instance of bad service we had but not about the dozens and dozens of instances of good service we had before that.

Even though we can be biased toward the negative, we still have a choice. We can't stop ourselves from feeling pain, but we can decide how much focus to place on that feeling versus all the other things we feel. We can choose where we sit energetically. We can choose whether we want to spend more of our time sitting in our happiness, gratitude, and love or whether we prefer to sit in our pain. Choosing the former changes everything.

By saying this, I'm not suggesting that you cut yourself off from feeling the range of human emotions, even the uglier ones. You can feel them—you *will* feel them. Nor am I suggesting this is easy. It's not. But it is possible to choose to allow pain less space in your life. Even when you're not sure how to do that, it can help just to know that it's possible.

When my grandmother passed away, it broke me in two. The loss was so painful for me that I didn't think I could carry it. I dropped everything in my life because I felt like I couldn't function. I couldn't even bring myself to go to her funeral because I didn't feel like I could handle being there with all those people to say goodbye.

When I was in the midst of that life-shattering pain, I felt like I was never going to get past it. But there was one thought that helped me break through it, even if it was just a crack at first. That thought was this: I didn't want the pain of my grandmother's loss to drown out all the good I'd received from her throughout my lifetime—all the important things I'd learned from her and all the many loving moments I'd had with her. It was really important to me that that didn't happen. I didn't know how I was going to do it yet, but I knew that I wanted to honor her love, not continue to sit with my pain. Because I couldn't have both. When I was consumed with so much pain, I couldn't *feel* my love for her. And I wanted to feel it so badly. It forced me to choose.

REDIRECTING THE PAIN

Deciding that love is worth choosing over pain doesn't mean that your pain will magically disappear. What it does mean is that you have a reason to focus on your own healing instead of your pain. So how do you do that? What can you do to lighten the burden you're carrying? First, you can allow yourself to feel the pain. Then, when you're ready, you can start to shift it.

After my grandmother died, I felt stuck. I couldn't look ahead because it hurt too much to think about life without her. But I discovered that I could look back. I could look back at the amazing gifts she'd given me when she was alive. I went back in my mind to every moment I'd had with her—moments that still felt alive and well because they were still so relevant to me—and I used those memories as fuel for my healing. Even now, after several years have passed, I still do this. If I feel pain, I go back and revisit my best moments. I think about sitting in my grandmother's backyard under the fruit trees while she made food—like her étouffée, which was my favorite, or her pound cake, her German chocolate cake, her lemon cake, really any of her amazing cakes. I remember the conversations I had with her that helped me find my path in life and gave me a fuller understanding of the person I wanted to be. I do this not to ignore the pain, but to put it in perspective. Pain is just one of the many things I've felt. As often as I can, I choose to focus on bringing more feelings of connection, caring, and love to the forefront.

This is what I call "redirection." It's about accepting the energy of whatever you're feeling, and then choosing to move some of that energy—respectfully and with intention—to a more positive and empowering place.

Micro-gestures can be a powerful tool for helping you do this. For example, a woman came to Lunch On Me after a difficult breakup to help us give out food. She'd been feeling alone and rejected, and giving in this way opened up space for her to feel something different for a while—to feel connected to and accepted by others. Similarly, there was a woman who reached out to us after losing her job unexpectedly. She admitted that it had been a big hit to her self-esteem, but she didn't want to just sit at home and feel useless. So she came out to be of use and to be around people who understood what she was feeling.

Of course, micro-gestures aren't going to solve all your problems—that first woman was still on her own, and the other was still unemployed—but micro-gestures can help us put our feelings into perspective. They can remind us that the negative things we feel about ourselves and our lives aren't the only things we're capable of feeling. If we can gradually shift, or redirect, more and more of our energy to a more positive place as we work through our problems, then that's how we can heal.

Throughout most of our journey together so far, I've focused on using our gifts to help people who have been forgotten, whether that's people who don't have a home, foster children, the sick and injured, or so many others. There are reasons for that. For one, I believe in starting where there is the greatest need—where love is the most absent. But there is another reason, which is that it can often be easier to offer help and care to strangers because they don't carry with them the same baggage that accompanies our closest relationships. We can use that to our advantage. When we feel ourselves shutting down or closing off our hearts because we've been hurt by someone close to us, we can practice opening our hearts back up in situations that are less emotionally charged. We can help our hearts build strength in this way and remind ourselves of our innate power to give to and care for others. Creating small moments though micro-gestures can be a way of gradually opening ourselves up to more love so that when we're ready, we can choose to sit with that energy rather than with our pain.

REDIRECTION: A DEFINITION

Noun. Accepting the energy of the moment, and then starting to move that energy, shifting it to a more positive and empowering place.

TAKE TIME TO HEAL . . . REGULARLY

Those closest to us have a way of pressing on our pain points, which can get in the way of love. We can't help that, but we can help how sensitive we are to the pressure. After all, there's a big difference between an open wound and a scar. So many people keep their wounds open instead of allowing them to heal, but when we heal, we become much more resilient. A scar may serve as a reminder of a past hurt, but it can still withstand a lot more impact than a fresh wound.

This is why it's important to take time to heal regularly. Not just when a traumatic event happens, but every day. For me, this too is part of the discipline of love. It's part of the discipline of loving ourselves and also of expanding our capacity to love others.

I didn't start doing this until a few years ago, after my grandmother had passed. You can probably tell by now that that was a life-changing time for me in a lot of ways. One of those ways came in the form of a realization about how much pain I was already carrying. The pain of my grandmother's loss was just so intense that I couldn't carry anything else. It was all-consuming, so I suddenly found myself in a position of having to figure out what to do about all the past wounds that were weighing me down because I'd never allowed them to heal. I could no longer shoulder all the burdens at once, not anymore, not with this new pain piled on top of them. So I had to let go of old baggage.

I think of it in the same way that I think about carrying extra pounds. Not only was I in pain after my grandmother died, but I also gained weight, which is probably why I see a correlation. The weight gain happened, in all likelihood, because I wasn't getting out and being as active as I once had been and because I sometimes turned to food for comfort. But it built up so gradually that I barely even noticed it happening. It felt like, all of a sudden, I woke up and had this extra weight that I was carrying with me everywhere I went.

Emotional pain can be very much the same. It can build up so slowly that we hardly even notice it. That is, until it gets to a critical point where it feels like it's really weighing us down or holding us back. Either that, or something big happens in our life—like the loss of someone close to us—that takes up most of our energy. That's when we might realize just how much energy we've unconsciously been putting toward protecting old wounds.

This is why I now make a point of giving my pain time and space on a regular basis to heal. I've found that it's a lot easier to release my pain bit by bit than all at once, especially during a difficult period in my life.

Different people have different rituals for this. Some may journal or walk in nature to give themselves time and space to contemplate what they're feeling and heal the wounds that are calling for attention. I personally use what I've talked about before, which is my morning check-in time. It's quiet time that I take for myself every day, but now I've added some more things to think about when I do it. I like to light some incense to signal my intention for the moment. Then I close my eyes, check in with my heart, and ask myself some key questions:

How is my heart doing?

What old wounds am I still carrying?

What have I let go of?

What do I still need to let go of?

I also make a point of asking myself these questions when something triggers me or I find myself reacting in an unexpected way—if I start crying out of nowhere, for example. I now make myself do this rather than pushing past or ignoring the moment.

I really believe in the value of having rituals for this, tools that we become familiar with so that we can turn to them when life gets hard. I recently saw *A Beautiful Day in the Neighborhood*, the film about Mr. Rogers, and I was surprised to find that he talks quite a bit about this subject. In it, he's talking with a reporter who has noticed that people seem to line up to tell Mr. Rogers their problems. The reporter notes that that must be quite a burden to carry, and he wants to know how Mr. Rogers handles it.

"There is no normal life that's free from pain," Mr. Rogers replies.

"How do you deal with that?" the reporter asks.

"There are many ways you can deal with your feelings without hurting yourself or anyone else."

"Like what?"

"Well, you can pound a lump of clay. Or swim as fast as you can. Or play the lowest keys on the piano all at the same time."[3]

These weren't just idle suggestions. Mr. Rogers, a regular swimmer and amateur piano player, did these things in his day-to-day life to help him process his emotions. He even wrote a song about it, which he would sing on his show to help children understand what to do with their negative feelings.

It's an endearing song, but this isn't just kids' stuff. It's not just children who need to figure out what to do with the mad that they feel so they can move on from their pain. It was during my morning check-ins that I realized there was an angry part of me still waiting for an apology from my birth mom for the way she'd mistreated me. It was also during those quiet times when I realized something that would help me move on from that feeling: I deserved an apology, but I didn't have to wait for one. Instead, I could learn to say sorry to myself.

We can all take into our own hands the power to give ourselves what we need and long for. In fact, we should. When I realized I could apologize to myself for what my birth mom had put me through, it made so much sense to me. Of course I couldn't wait for her to make things right. Of course I wasn't going to get my healing from the same place where I got my pain. I had to be the source of my own healing. We all do if we want to be able to move on from our pain and focus more of our attention and energy on love.

We could all use more stillness in our lives—more time to think about what we feel and space to process what has happened to us. Whatever that looks like to you, make it a regular habit. Small changes can have big impacts, and a person can be delivered in this way from pain.

So what's your ritual? What do you do for yourself to help you work through your emotions and aid your healing? Is it a morning walk when you check in with your heart? Is it weekly therapy with a professional? Do you bang on piano keys when you need to exorcize difficult feelings, or talk them out with your best friend?

If you haven't already done so, take some time to explore what works best for you and then be intentional about carving out regular time in your schedule for it—every day, if possible.

REDIRECTING OTHER PEOPLE'S ENERGY

Of course, you can have a pretty good handle on your pain. You can be disciplined about love, bringing it into all your encounters with people. You can do all that, and you'll still have some awful encounters. That's because we are only one part of the equation in any exchange. We can do our best to make sure we don't bring any negative energy into our interactions, but we can't stop other people from bringing it.

Still, that doesn't leave us powerless. We can't stop negative energy from coming our way, but we can redirect it in ways similar to those we used earlier in this chapter to redirect our own pain, which will then allow us to bring love into the equation. It's important to learn how to do this because so many people only want to hold onto love when it's good. Too many people are quick to throw it away when all it needs is some extra effort and care. It's like the people who have volunteered with LOM to feed our wildflowers, had one bad experience, and then decided they never wanted to try again.

Or how about friends, workmates, even family members whom we find difficult to talk to or be around. Rather than doing anything about it, we might choose to avoid them or ghost them. Or we might opt to suck it up and deal with them in the moment, but complain about them later and regret the time we spent together. Like I said, you can't stop people from being who they are, but you can decide what dynamics you're willing to allow in your interactions. If you do that, then you can redirect accordingly.

I once had a landlord who made it quite obvious that he was used to treating women as secondary to men. I was on the phone with him once, and he was being very condescending, speaking to me as if I were a child whom he could talk over and tell what to do. It was obviously not okay, but I wasn't about to meet his rudeness with more rudeness. Where would that leave either of us? What I wanted was for the two of us to be able to speak respectfully to each other now and in the future, so I stopped the conversation midway to say just that.

"I'm going to have to interrupt for a moment," I said to him. "I'm not on this phone to check you, but I do need you to check yourself. I've never been disrespectful to you, so there's no reason for you to speak to me that way. Now, I'm going to sit here for a moment and wait while you take responsibility for that. Take some time and just think about it. You don't have to say anything because I've already forgiven you for today. But know that this will never happen again. We will only talk respectfully to each other in the future or we won't talk at all."

He immediately changed his tone, and we've been good ever since. It really was that easy, and it worked in large part because I didn't yell at him. I didn't speak down to him like he'd been doing to me. I was direct but also calm, and I even spoke with kindness.

I believe that there are always two dialogues going on when a person is talking. There are the things the person is saying out loud, the voice dialogue, and then there are the things the person is saying in their mind, the head dialogue. You have to speak to both in order to really get through to someone and shift the dynamic. In this case, the words my landlord was saying to me weren't really that bad, but his tone suggested that he believed he needed to talk down to me in order to show his authority and gain respect. So if respect was what his head dialogue was telling him he needed, then I would give it to him. I respected him enough to tell him the truth, and I told him in a way that came across as respectful.

This goes back to the energy exchange. Every encounter between two people is characterized by the energy that flows between them. Before focusing on what you want to say or what you need to accomplish, first you need to speak to the person's energy (the head dialogue) if you really want to get through to him and make an impact.

This can mean saying to someone, "I can tell you're really upset with me right now," when you know the person is feeling that way but isn't saying it. Or if someone is angry and speaking to you with a raised voice, you can respond with deliberate calm in order to diffuse the energy. Anger feeds off of anger, so when you deny someone that energy in an encounter, it's often like pulling the plug. Or when I meet someone for the first time and I can tell the person is nervous, right away I will ask if we can hug hello instead of shaking hands. A hug can be a great redirection in this kind of situation because it's hard to stay nervous after that. It's a way of breaking through a barrier between you and someone else. As Shaianne's grandmother used to say (the woman who first taught me that I needed to be a better hugger): "Something as small as a hug can change the world daily."

Sometimes people think that responding to others with love and caring is a weakness, but it really isn't. It's a strength if you do it right. I'm not talking about letting people get away with yelling at you or patronizing you, and you saying nothing but "I love you" in return. I'm talking about having the courage and presence of mind to respond to whatever is happening in the moment truthfully and with compassion, for yourself and for the other person. And knowing that if the interaction could or should be going better, you have every right to say so and the power to make that kind of difference.

I also redirect energy by being clear about my intention. I didn't just tell my landlord to stop speaking to me in that way. I told him that my intention was for us to speak respectfully to one another from then on. To the person who is speaking to you out of anger, you might say something like, "I don't want to fight with you; I just want to get this right." To the person who is yelling because she feels disempowered, you might say, "I really want to listen to you, and that's hard to do when there's so much heightened energy."

We shouldn't assume that our good intentions are obvious to others, even to the people who know us well. We have to remember that people often respond to us based on their own assumptions and their own experiences, even their own pain, just like we do. So when you tell them that what you want most of all is for this encounter to go well for both of you, it may contradict what they assume are your negative intentions.

This may sound a bit scary at first. After all, a lot of people naturally avoid any kind of confrontation. But this is why it's important to get a handle on yourself first, to know how to redirect your own energy before you start to redirect others'. If you don't have the discipline within yourself to understand and respond to your own pain, then how can you respond to someone else's?

The more centered you are in your own energy, the easier it will be to redirect someone else's.

And like everything else, it will get easier the more you practice it. Another big lesson I've learned on Skid Row is that I'm capable of speaking kindly to a stranger even during tough encounters. So if I can do that with a stranger, how can I not do it with the people I love, even when they're being difficult? I've had plenty of practice keeping my cool on Skid Row, so all I have to do now is transfer that energy to situations at home.

It was that lesson that made me resolve to stop yelling and arguing with my brothers and sisters, as I've mentioned before. After all, it doesn't make sense for me to treat the people I'm most invested in worse than people I've just met. I think we can all agree that that's just not how love is supposed to work.

REMEMBER YOUR ACTS OF NON-RESISTANCE

Being able to accept the situations before us as they are, even if they're difficult or unpleasant, is key in being responsive rather than reactive. Responsiveness over reactiveness is what I call an act of non-resistance, and it allows us to learn so much more from difficult situations and do so much more to affect them in a positive way.

This is going to be a very important skill to make use of when you want to redirect someone's energy. When people make it difficult for you to bring the love, one of the best things you can do is *not* meet those people where they're at.

As I said before, my dad was my best example of this. He used to say to my birth mother when she was yelling at him (which she did a lot): "Please raise your words, not your voice." It always amazed me how calm he remained even in the face of her anger. Not me. Back then I was an angry mess, and not just at home. But my dad was always calm and accepting with me as well. I sometimes wonder if he hadn't been, if he had met my anger and frustration with anger and frustration of his own, where would I be today? That's another important thing you can do to bring compassion into difficult exchanges: remind yourself that you haven't always been easy to love, and yet there are people who persisted.

Not long ago my younger brother got married. He's only twenty-five, and he'd only known the woman he married for a couple of months. I thought it was a mistake, which is probably what he figured I'd say and the reason he didn't tell me in advance about their impromptu wedding at city hall. I found out about it when he changed his status to "married" on Facebook.

I told my brother the truth about what I thought of his relationship because I believe it's important to be honest with the people we love. But after that, I left it alone. After all, he hasn't done anything wrong. He hasn't done anything to me personally. And it's not my life. If he has made a mistake, then he's entitled. And if he decides he's made a mistake, then in order to fix it he's going to need the people who love him more than ever. And maybe he hasn't made a mistake. I have my opinion, which comes from my own experiences, but I'm not him. It's in times like these when it's a good idea to call on that humility that we talked about in chapter 5. We can never truly know what's best for another person because we haven't lived all their experiences and we're not in their heads. That's always going to be true, no matter how much we may like to think otherwise.

Whatever his reasons were, whatever the outcome of his marriage, I choose to keep my focus on what's most important, which is that I don't love my brother any differently now than I did before. His decision did cause some tension in our relationship, but I always think that if love is bigger than the problem you're facing, then choose love. If the problem is bigger, then maybe the relationship needs to go. In this case, the love is definitely bigger. My brother is still welcome in my life, as is his wife, as is anyone else he chooses to bring along. Because I love him through all his seasons. I love him through all his lessons. I love him no matter what.

It can be hard to hold back our opinions when we really want to express them. Or tamp down our anger when it's bubbling to the surface. Or redirect our pain when it might feel really good in the moment to just lash out. This is where one of the most powerful lessons I learned on Skid Row can help. The people who live there are constantly under pressure. They're insulted, looked down on, deprived, ignored, even attacked on a regular basis. They're constantly having salt rubbed on their open wounds, with so few moments of peace, so little support to help them heal. And yet, most of them, most of the time are able to maintain their composure in the midst of it all. When I feel like losing it, I remind myself of their example. If there are people out there who can keep it together under the toughest of circumstances, then why can't I?

A lot of times the negative ways we interact with people are just bad habits. Acts of non-resistance give us a chance to disrupt the habit, so we have a chance to replace it with something new that will better support the kind of loving relationships we want. In this way, we can set the tone for love, not just for ourselves, but for the people around us. And that's what the next chapter is about.

❤ HEARTWORK ❤

If you're struggling in one of your relationships, take some time to consider the following questions.

Ask yourself: *Is the love I have for this person bigger than the problem we're facing? Or is the problem bigger?*

If it's the first one, then choose love, even if you haven't yet worked out what that means for the relationship. You can still decide that love is going to be your primary focus, and let that guide you as you work through the problem. If the problem is bigger, then maybe it's time to let the relationship go.

8

RESET WITH YOUR TRIBE

"One man cannot change the world, but you and I can change the world together. You and I have to find out what is truth; for it is truth that dissolves the sorrows, the miseries of the world."

JIDDU KRISHNAMURTI, *Indian philosopher*[1]

Years ago, before I started LOM, I fed people quietly on my own. I told my grandmother about what I was doing when I was living with her as a teenager, but I didn't talk about it to anyone else. I never even told my friends until one November when my friend Meg asked me what I was doing for Thanksgiving. It seemed silly to lie to her, so I told her, a bit shyly, that I was going to stay home and cook a bunch of food. Then I was going to bring it to people who needed it.

"I want to do that too!" she said right away. I was surprised, but I said okay. She was so excited that she started telling other people, and pretty soon a whole group of our friends were making plans to shop, cook, and distribute food together. They were my first volunteers, and we had the best time. Practically everyone commented on what a memorable day it was and how glad they were to be there. A month later I was still receiving texts asking, "When can we do that again!?!"

I suddenly found myself wondering why I hadn't done this before. Feeding people was one of the greatest joys in my life, so why was I keeping it to myself?

There's a real opportunity for people who learn how to Love Without Reason to share their discoveries with those closest to them—their neighbors, their coworkers, their friends, their children, their spouses, their extended family members. After all, we all need love. We may not all have the same needs as my

Skid Row street family, but we all need love to be given to us and we all need ways to express the love we have inside.

That's what this chapter is for. I'll talk about some of the ways you can spread the LWR spirit to the people closest to you, so you can share the joy with them—for their sake as well as your own.

OPEN UP YOUR TRIBE

I've seen micro-gestures really change people, one small act at a time. One of the reasons why they work so well is that you don't have to change your life to do them. You can be going about your normal, daily routine, and simply look at the world through a slightly different lens—one that takes more notice of the people around you and how you can impact them in a positive way. LWR isn't something for which you have to redirect your life. It's something you can incorporate into your life as it already is.

When you're thinking about bringing LWR to your tribe members, think about tweaking your perspective in a similar way. Consider being a little more open and inclusive about who gets to be in your tribe.

After all, our tribe is (or should be) our chosen family. It may include our blood relations, but it doesn't have to. I'm living proof that shared DNA doesn't make you any closer to someone. I'm close to all seven of my siblings, but that's because I love their spirits. I choose to have them in my life, but my chosen family doesn't include all my family members. My birth mom is no longer in my life, as I've said before. My birth father isn't either. The man I call dad, my birth mom's ex-husband, is one of the most important people in my life, but he has no blood relationship to me at all.

TRIBE: A DEFINITION

Noun. Your chosen circle of people or your chosen family. Not the people you were born to, but those whom you choose to keep and do this walk with.

More important than sticking with the people we're born to is surrounding ourselves with people who support our values. This is another way we can take responsibility for bringing more love into our lives: we can choose people who help us feel more loving and more loved.

I think of my friend Ms. Tanya. We met when I was only twenty-one years old. I had just broken up with the first big love of my life, Jai, who had played a huge role in my life up to that point. She was the person who gave me the courage to run from my birth mother when I was still conflicted about abandoning a family member, even though that person stepped on me every day. Jai had been there for me when I finally started to let go, and when we broke up, I felt adrift, vulnerable, and alone.

This happened at a time when I was an actor and performer, which was how I ended up at an audition for a new play. The scene I was told to prepare was a monologue in which a young woman is talking about being deeply in love with a person she has to let go of. Unbelievably, the man whom the character was missing so deeply was named Jai.

It was the perfect outlet for all the feelings I was carrying but didn't know how to express. I showed up at the audition, where I knew no one, and just poured all my energy into the performance. When I finished, I looked up and saw the woman who had written the play sitting in front of me bawling her eyes out. She got up from her chair and walked over to me. Without saying a word, she enveloped me in a hug. At that point in my life, I wasn't used to having such intimate moments with strangers, but I just went with it. Soon after she closed the auditions and invited me to sit with her for a chat.

This is how I was first introduced to Ms. Tanya. We sat there together for a while afterward talking about our lives. She told me she had written the play about her own relationship and had been struck to see how much my emotions mirrored her own, which made her want to get to know me better. I had never met anyone so genuinely open and honest before. I was a little bit confused by it at first, but I also wanted more of it. Ms. Tanya and I started meeting regularly for dinner after that.

That was more than a decade ago, and we've been friends ever since. We meet every year for dinner to celebrate our birthdays together like we would if we were family—and in my heart, we are. She has not only been a great friend to me, but also a teacher. Her example taught me to become more open and honest with all people (not just the ones I'm close to) like she is, and she knows how to nudge me in the right direction when I need a push. Sometimes I think about how easy it would have been to turn away from her back then because I wasn't used to accepting love from strangers. I'm so thankful that I didn't.

EXPOSURE IS BETTER THAN CONVERSION

The biggest mistake I think people make when it comes to sharing something important to them is that they try to convert rather than expose. It's like when someone finds religion and then suddenly comes knocking on your door to tell you that you should believe the same things he or she does. The tactic generally works only with those who already have a similar mindset.

When you want to share what you've experienced, it's best not to start from the perspective of "I'm going to change this person." Instead you can tell yourself, "Let me show people the change in me and see what happens." It's a matter of teaching people through your actions instead of telling them what to do. After all, who likes to be told that what they're doing or thinking or believing is wrong? No one, that's who.

I was confronted with this fact when I decided several years ago that I wanted to introduce healthy foods to my family. My siblings and I didn't grow up with the best eating habits, and we were never really taught to think about how the foods we chose affected our health. We just ate what was available and tasted good. After I left home, I became a vegan and felt so much better physically and mentally as a result. I wanted my siblings to feel as good as I did, so I started pressuring them to eat differently. Well, of course it failed. And not only did it fail, but I annoyed them in the process. I had to back off. Now, I simply invite them over and make delicious, healthy food for us to share, the same kinds of things that I eat myself or share with people on Skid Row. I don't preach veganism any longer. In fact, I don't talk about it at all unless someone asks. We just enjoy the food together, and gradually I've watched as their willingness to try more and more healthy options has grown. If you let people see your journey, sometimes that will inspire them to go on one too.

While it's best to avoid preaching to your loved ones, it's just as important not to hide from them. If you're making big changes in your life or you're engaging in new activities that are important to you, then it's perfectly okay to share what's going on. In fact, if you don't share, you're probably not being truly open and honest in your relationships.

This means just being yourself, even if that means being a slightly different version of yourself in front of people who have known you for a long time and may find it a bit unfamiliar. For example, if you've gotten into the habit of doing micro-gestures when you're out and about, don't stop just because you're with your mother or your childhood best friend. Do your micro-gestures in the same way that you would if no one else was watching. And then let what happens happen.

You might find, like I did that Thanksgiving Day, that your friends and family have been waiting for something like this to come into their lives. If that's their reaction, then you'll likely get some questions about it. That's your signal that it's a good time to explain what you're doing and why.

If you do find that someone is curious or inspired, then you can respond with an open invitation to join you. After I talked about micro-gestures during my interview with Tal Rabinowitz (whom I mentioned in chapter 3), she wondered why she wasn't doing it more. Not long after, she had picked up her preschool-age daughter from dance class, and they were headed to the donut shop for a treat. They passed a man across the street who looked like he was homeless. Because she had her daughter with her and the guy looked to be packing up his things so he could move on, she said she probably wouldn't have approached him before out of a fear that she might be bothering him. But after we talked, she decided to just try to connect and see what happened.

"Hey, my daughter and I are going to get donuts," she said to him. "Would you like one?"

"I'd love a coffee," he replied.

"Why not both—coffee and a donut?" she asked.

He agreed and thanked her profusely. Tal then asked him how he took his coffee and what kind of donut he would like.

"His smile was getting progressively bigger as we talked," she remembered. Her daughter had been watching this the whole time but hadn't said much. When they went back to bring the man his coffee and donut, Tal told him to have a nice day and started to walk away. Then her daughter turned toward him with the biggest smile on her face, waved at him, and yelled it too: "Have a nice daaaay!!!"

Tal's young daughter seemed to really enjoy the interaction, so they started doing it more and more often. It's now a kind of ritual that they do together: go out and get food and share some of it with whoever is around and might want some. It's become such a regular habit that her daughter now expects it to be part of all her outings, even when she's with her dad and Tal isn't there.

I think most people with children hope that their kids will grow up to become caring, generous, and empathetic people, but those qualities don't just appear out of nowhere. Micro-gestures can be a great way of modeling these things for children, starting at a very young age, so they can begin to see the world through caring eyes. Because they are simple and easy to do, micro-gestures are also great things to invite kids of any age to participate in. Ask them what they would like to do for others and what gifts they might have to share. I knew someone who took her daughter to a toy drive that had been set up to provide holiday presents to a local foster home. Her daughter was curious about what was going to happen to all the toys, so she explained that there were some kids out there who didn't get anything for the holidays.

After that, the daughter decided she wanted to give away half the new toys she got for all her birthdays and Christmases to the foster home. It was empowering for her to be able to choose, and she loved doing it.

While it obviously won't be quite the same as with kids, I actually think that empathy, caring, and generosity are great qualities for us to model for anyone of any age. Of course, not everyone will take to your example as quickly and easily—or sometimes even at all—as Tal's daughter did, but that's okay. When you share with people, you have to be okay with them having opinions, whether positive or negative or even ambivalent. This is really just another chance to practice your non-resistance. However people respond to your displays of love, just accept it. Their reaction will be based on their own past experiences and how open they are. This means it's not about what you're doing so much as it's about where they are in their lives. Let them be where they need to be.

TAKE PEOPLE AS THEY ARE

Choosing exposure over a more heavy-handed approach is really about staying humble. Just because something works for us doesn't mean it will work—or work in the same way—for someone else. And just because we're ready for change doesn't mean those around us are ready at the same time. Loving people means loving them for who and where they are in their lives.

When you've practiced love so often that it becomes second nature to you, you have to remember to be more gracious toward others who haven't had the same experience. Everyone is on their own path toward healing, learning, and growth. If you want people to respect your path and give you the space to make your own choices and mistakes along the way, then you have to do the same for them.

When someone questions what we're doing or even rejects the changes in us, then we just need to remember that their reaction is not about us. The people who don't accept loving gestures are not really rejecting us; they're responding to a world that has hurt them. Wanting to give and receive love is a natural instinct. That's why we see it in children who have just entered this world. That's why it's something that transcends language, culture, and geography. Still, you can't expect everyone to be ready for love when you are. As time goes on, you'll come to see that when someone isn't ready to accept your love, or accept you as a more loving person, then it's just a sign that they have more work to do on themselves.

All we can do is respect that and keep on loving them. This is the steeping, the hanging in there and continuing to choose love, even when it's hard.

Even if people aren't ready to accept love in the moment, you can still plant a seed. You can give that person a different type of experience to take with them, something to counteract the experiences that have closed them off or are holding them back.

When someone rejects love, I always see it as an expression of their pain. I can empathize with them because I've had plenty of my own pain that I've had to move past in order to have more loving relationships with people. This idea of acknowledging others' pain is important to keep in mind as you work through your own pain, like we talked about in the last chapter. Because we've all been hurt in one way or another, our pain can be something that connects us. We may not know exactly what someone else has been through, but we can usually recognize pain when we see it because we've all been there before. And when we can identify with someone's pain—even (or especially) if that person is different than us or even (or especially) if that person is rejecting us—then it opens up room for us to try to understand them. That's what respect really is—admitting that we can't understand everything about another person but we can make an effort to try just a little bit harder because we can empathize with where someone might be coming from. Otherwise we get stuck in a judgment trap where we focus only on the problem or disagreement and not the possibilities for a solution. Mother Teresa said, "If you judge people, you have no time to love them."

For example, when I talk about LOM, people say things all the time about how they believe that the homeless have chosen that life, that they want to live as they do, so why should they help them? This reaction is common, but it's also based on a lack of experience and understanding. I know homelessness is not a choice because I've had the experience of getting to know a lot of different people who live on the street. Judging someone for thinking otherwise isn't going to inspire that person to change. Instead, if we take time to understand where someone is coming from, then we can respond in a loving and nurturing way. But the understanding has to come first.

This is why, in the previous chapter, I talked about the importance of healing our own pain. It's what will create space for empathy and understanding to come into our relationships. Otherwise, we're too focused on our own hurt to make any progress with other people. Let's face it: if you look hard enough, you can find a reason to judge every person you meet and a reason to reject every person you know. Of course, others can do the same to us. If that's the perspective we all choose, then we're all going to end up feeling pretty lonely.

Even when people won't grant us a better understanding of themselves, we can still respect the fact that there's so much about why they are the way they are that we simply don't know. When it comes to things that can really set us off, like political or religious differences, it helps to keep this in mind. Even when we know for absolute certain that someone is wrong, we can remember that we all learn our lessons in different seasons. If our instinct instead is to right the wrong, place blame, shame the person who made the mistake, then we've got bigger problems than what's happening in front of us. If that's our instinct, it means we're not remembering all the times we've been wrong too. It also means we're not seeing clearly that judging people is never going to help enlighten them; it's only going to invite judgment back on ourselves. When someone is in pain—and I consider ignorance a kind of pain—then the only thing that's going to help is caring, understanding, and love.

Remember, we're at a point where we're looking to steep in love so that we can master it, so the next time someone tells you who they voted for in the presidential election and you just want to scream, take it as an opportunity to stretch yourself, to be more open, to practice the third of the three Be's that you need to LWR: Be generous. These moments aren't about the other person. They're about us and our own expansion. Loving people isn't easy, so dare yourself to love people through your biggest disagreements and even through their darkest seasons.

And have the courage to show them who you're becoming. I've changed a lot since that Thanksgiving Day when I finally told my friends about my habit of feeding people. Now I invite people to come with me all the time—friends, family, neighbors, strangers, anyone who's interested. I invite people, but importantly, I invite them with no expectations and no attachments. If they come, great. If they don't, fine.

LOM is a community-based organization. We try to make clear through our programs and social media that everyone is welcome. Often friends who have never volunteered before, or haven't for a long time, will show up after a breakup, the loss of a job, a period of illness, or some other difficult life event. They do it to feel better about themselves, and they wind up helping others in the process.

I never judge anyone's reasons for showing up because I don't think it matters why we do good things. I just think it matters that we do them and allow ourselves to be changed by them. It may be true that we each have our own path to follow, but none of us wants to be on the journey alone. If we can allow other people to be exactly who they are in this and every moment, then we will have a lot more company as we move through this life.

LOVE IS A COLLABORATION AND A CELEBRATION

As I said in the previous chapter, we can love people from afar if we have to, and we may have to if they don't treat us well. We can also continue to love someone who is distant and doesn't yet know how to receive love. Even when it feels one-sided, I don't believe that the energy of love is wasted. When you put love into the world, it doesn't always come back to you right away, but I do believe it has a positive impact.

At its best, however, love is a collaboration. It's a give and take, an exchange of energy, so if the loving energy can be maximized on both sides, imagine what a difference that could make.

I met a woman not long ago who had recently come back from a silent retreat. She described it as a liberating experience, but she was struggling with how to make the experience last. She didn't want everything she'd learned there to be left at the retreat's door, so she was trying to figure out how, as she described it, "to embed the lessons in my relationships."

"I think that's the best way to integrate what I learned into my life," she told me.

I agreed with her. When we can create change within ourselves, and then express those changes in our relationships—especially the ones that have been part of our lives for a long time—that's when we know we're on our way to really mastering something. It's a further exercise of our discipline that can have a positive effect on us, on those around us, and on our relationships with those people. After all, imagine if you and your spouse, or best friend, or sibling, both became masters of love. How much better might life be if you were masters together?

I like to integrate Love Without Reason into my relationships by creating opportunities to celebrate the people I love. One of the things I've done is institute a tradition of what I call "appreciation dinners." Once a month or so, I'll gather the people I love together—family members, people I work with, friends—and I'll cook for them or take them out. I don't wait for holidays or birthdays. I make it clear to them that I want to take the opportunity to celebrate them because I love them and I'm so happy they're in my life.

You can do this in any number of different ways. Schedule more one-on-one time with the people you care about or send them gifts out of the blue. Write people notes telling them what they mean to you or just saying that you're thinking about them because they're so important to you. Everyone likes to be thought of. What it comes down to is asking yourself what you want the people you care about to encounter when they encounter you. And then act accordingly to bring that feeling into the relationship.

For the woman who wanted to make the most out of her silent retreat, she can certainly talk to her friends about how much the experience meant to her (while avoiding the suggestion that this is what *they* need in their lives too—remember, no one likes to be preached to with unsolicited opinions). But more than that, she can bring the lessons she learned into her relationships through her own example. When she's with someone, she can put her phone away in order to focus on the conversation. When a friend is talking, she can listen closely without jumping in, interrupting, or thinking about what she wants to say next. She can avoid the impulse to fill a silent moment with unnecessary talk. In every moment she has with someone, she can practice being calm, responsive, and in the moment. That energy will have an effect on people—whether they consciously notice it or not, whether they talk about it or not—because we all respond to energy.

There are endless ways to bring more loving energy into our relationships, but they all require us to be more attentive to people rather than treating them like they're always going to be there. I heard a woman say the other day that she hadn't talked to her best friend in months, but it didn't matter; they'd been friends for years so she knew her friend would always be there to pick up where they left off when she found the time to reach out to her.

This sentiment frustrates me. I feel the same way when someone says, "You know that I love you." I always want the person on the receiving end of that statement to say, "No, I don't. Why don't you tell me? Or better yet, show me?" You're not being loving if people have to guess whether you care about them. And it's not loving to assume they'll always be there when you want them to be. It's also just not true. People can change or move on, especially if they're feeling neglected.

Sometimes I think that the hardest thing about love isn't getting through the hard times; it's all the times when it would be easy to take love for granted. Choosing not to, choosing to keep love top of mind, even when there's nothing calling your immediate attention to it, is where we can really exercise our discipline.

This is what I do with my best friend, Jamila. We've been close since we were five years old, when I was living in Spanish Harlem and she would visit her aunts on the weekends who lived just up the street from me. She still lives on the East Coast, while I live in Los Angeles, so it would be easy to let our relationship lapse. But she's too important for that. Because it would be easy to neglect the relationship, I make an extra effort to contact her regularly and create an active line of communication. Even during the busiest times in our lives, I'll send her a text saying: "I know your life is crazy right now. Mine is too. But I still wanted to check in with you because I love you so much!"

Because we are lifelong collaborators in this relationship, she does the same to me. Because I'm not perfect. I get caught up in life, too, and don't always remember what's most important. We've talked about how important it is to not let our relationship stagnate, but to instead keep the love flowing, so we pick up the slack for each other when one of us falters. And I gratefully accept her loving gestures whenever they come my way, which is just as important in a collaboration. Sometimes people will be happy to give, but they're uncomfortable receiving things from others, whether it's gifts, compliments, or just expressions of love. Some people will even consider themselves generous when they insist on being the only giver in a relationship, but this really isn't generous at all. It's just another way of cutting off the reciprocal energy of love, the give and the take. How can it be considered loving to deny someone the chance to express their love and caring to you?

At the end of the day, what I want most is for my love to be unquestionable. Undoubtable. When my grandmother died, I knew without even the edge of a question that she loved me wholly, and I want the people I love to feel the same way. I mentioned before that I didn't go to her funeral because it was too painful. Another reason is that I really dislike funerals in general because they always feel like misplaced energy to me. People show up to them with their flowers and kind words, which always makes me think how much better it would have been if the person were still alive to receive them. The only moment we're guaranteed to have with the people we love is this one right now, so take advantage of it.

♥ HEARTWORK ♥

Ask yourself: *What feeling do I want people to have when they encounter me?*

Then ask yourself: *What am I doing in my current relationships to make sure that happens?*

GENUINE SHARING

One of the best ways to have a positive effect on our tribe is by being more conscious of what we're putting into the world for them to see and experience. For example, I love social media, and it's played a huge role in building a community to support LOM. But we're careful about what we put on social media platforms because we know it's yet another way that we infuse our energy into the world. This is why we don't spend a lot of time hyping ourselves and our accomplishments. Instead we focus on celebrating our street family, with colorful photos of them, videos of them dancing or singing, callouts about their artwork or poetry, or just messages about how happy we were to see them that day.

I think we could all take more responsibility for what we share with our tribe (or with the world if our platform is that large). Instead of Instagramming a photo of what you had for lunch today, how about highlighting your acts of service? Instead of Tweeting a complaint about the latest political headline, how about telling a story about someone whose voice deserves to be heard? You can share with others how you're GAF each and every day, and make acts of love your public protest against an uncaring world.

I understand that this can be tough sometimes and that genuine sharing can make a person feel vulnerable. It's been only about a year that I've been speaking publicly about our work at LOM, and the first time I was invited to do it, I was completely thrown by it. I didn't talk much when I was growing up, so I couldn't understand why someone would suddenly want to hand me a microphone. The idea made me feel so self-conscious, and I was worried that I'd sound like an idiot, or worse, like one of those arrogant people who loves to hear themselves talk. I even tried to get Ms. Tanya to write the speech for me, but she said no because she knew I needed to do it myself.

Finally, after a lot of angst about it, I realized that the best thing to do was to just speak from my heart. I was never going to be a perfect public speaker, but I did have something to say that I was passionate about. I figured that if God gives you the room, you better make sure you're talking about something that matters. That simple idea has guided me ever since.

I think it's an idea that can guide us all, no matter what our platform is—social media, a conference stage, a network television show with millions of viewers, or a group of friends hanging out and talking. The venue doesn't matter as much as what we choose to say. And we can all choose to speak more often about things that matter.

We can also choose to speak more truth. When I freed myself from the idea that I needed to be perfect, it made the idea of giving a talk in front of a live audience feel so much more appealing. When you look back at that speech, I don't look perfect, I don't sound perfect, I stumbled through some of my words, but my emotions were real and they came through. I could tell, because when I ended the speech with a story close to my heart about one of the people we had helped on Skid Row, the audience was crying along with me.

One of the greatest gifts I think we can bring to our tribe is our willingness to be truly open and honest despite all the messiness that can come with that. Can we look where it hurts and have real conversations about what we see there with the people we love? Can we invite people to see us in all our imperfections and to be just as imperfect in front of us without our judgment? Can we have the courage to bring more of our focus to the things that really matter? It feels so freeing to be able to do this for ourselves, and so empowering and reassuring to be able to do it together and for each other.

I hope you understand by now that this book isn't just about curing our homeless problem; it's about addressing all the world's wounds to the best of our abilities. To do that, we have to remember what I said before: we don't need to change the world by ourselves. The more the merrier, because not only are we more powerful together, it's also more fun and meaningful to give a f♥ck together. So remember to do your part, and then empower those around you to do the same through your example.

And then go as big as your collective hearts will allow. When I founded LOM, I started with my own neighborhood, but now we've been in Detroit, New York, Hawaii, Miami, Texas, and more. And I want to keep going. Someday I'd even like to go global. And why not? With a big enough community to support the idea, there's nothing to stop us.

9

KEEP CHOOSING THE LIGHT

*"There are no bad days. Only days when you have
to look harder to find the light."*

JOHNNIE GASTON

Johnnie Gaston was my grandmother's name, and she used to say this to me all the time when I was young. From her I learned that perspective is everything. The perspective that I try to remind myself of every day, no matter what's happening in my life, is this: We all have something that someone else in this world is praying for right now. We have food while someone else is hungry. We have shelter while someone else is exposed. We have company while someone else is lonely. We have love while someone else is hated or ignored.

As we wind up this book, I want to talk a little bit about adopting a perspective that will sustain you as you move forward with love and a giving heart. There are a lot of things in life that we don't have much control over, but our perspective isn't one of them. We can always choose to see things differently. It can be hard sometimes to look for the light, but it's always there. And though it's hard sometimes, it's absolutely worth the effort.

CHOOSE ACCOUNTABILITY

We can choose to look for the light, even on days when it's hard to do, if we hold ourselves accountable. Accountability means being honest with ourselves. We have to look at why we do what we do, not with a sense of judgment, but with curiosity and a desire for self-correction and growth.

I once saw an elderly man on the sidewalk who had fallen and couldn't get up. People were stepping right over him as they continued on their way. I walked over to ask if he was okay, and he had tears in his eyes when I did. "I was beginning to think that no one cared about me at all, and that I'd have to stay down here forever," he said. It broke my heart that someone would be made to feel that way just because he'd fallen down.

It's times like these when we really have to look at where it hurts and ask ourselves the hard questions: What is it inside us that allows us to walk past someone who is suffering? What makes us not want to help someone when we could? This isn't what we were born to do. Children don't walk past someone like that and pretend not to see him, not until they're taught to by adults. So why do we?

Truth is one of the hardest things we have to face in this life—the truth about ourselves most of all. But that truth isn't something we should be afraid or ashamed of. Truth is just another form of light. When we can see things clearly, when we can shed light upon them, that's when we'll know how to make things better.

CHOOSE ACTION

Accountability isn't supposed to be paralyzing. It's supposed to be inspiring. It's our launching pad, our starting point for learning and growing and changing.

After all, we're all figuring things out as we go along. That's just how life is. Not long ago, I was in New York, where I used to live, coordinating an event to promote Lunch On Me. An old roommate found out that I'd be in town and wanted to get together. Because my schedule was so packed, I invited her to come to the event to help out.

LOM had a booth at a local coffee festival, which is where she met me. We hung out as people stopped to buy LWR tees and hats and learn more about what we do. I was talking to someone about how many former foster kids we serve when we're on Skid Row, and my friend was listening. When the person left, my friend said to me, "I could have easily become one of those kids you feed. I was abandoned when I was a baby, but then I was adopted by my parents, who are really good people and gave me everything I needed. It was nothing but luck that I ended up with them instead of in foster care. And even still, I never give back. I can't believe how shitty I've been."

I've seen this before. Someone will notice me helping others and decide that makes me "good." Then they realize they don't do what I do, so they must be "bad." They start to get down on themselves, which stops them from trying to do something about it. And it all spirals downward from there.

It's a trap that we all need to look out for. We can devote so much energy to putting ourselves down that we don't have anything left over to give. When this happens, it's a good time to remember what my grandmother said and look a little harder to find the light.

This isn't about being a good or bad person. Remember, we all learn our lessons in our own time, and my old roommate happened to be learning one that day. It was up to her to decide what to do about it. She could feel bad about herself and become paralyzed as a result. Of course, in the long run that would only make her feel worse because she would continue to be a "shitty" person, by her own definition. Or she could choose to shift her perspective to something else. That's a shift we can always choose to make. Instead of focusing on what we've done wrong in the past, we can choose to think about what we can do right now—no matter how small—to help someone else feel better.

WHY I GIVE A F♥CK . . .

"I care about people, not because they deserve it, but because it's what God expects of me. I love people, not because they know how to love, but because we are mandated by God to love ALL things."

TANYA
CFO, age 60

CHOOSE CELEBRATION

I also suggested to my old roommate that she celebrate the moment. She had learned something about herself. She had caught a glimpse of new possibilities for herself and for her life. Those moments don't happen all the time. Instead of feeling bad that the realization hadn't dawned on her before, why not be glad that it did right now?

I believe we need more celebrating in our lives, more celebrations of our growth and of the gifts we've shared. People spend too much time waiting for the big moments to come along. It happens all the time with volunteering. I get tons of inquiries from people who want to help out on Thanksgiving and Christmas, but I usually take the big holidays off because I know it's when the rest of the world is paying attention. It's the other 363 days of the year, the quiet days when fewer people are paying attention, when help is really needed.

Too many people are looking for change to come in the form of some grand, theatrical moment, but that's not how it usually works. In my experience, change is more often the result of tiny whispers followed by small moments that build, one on top of the other, over time. An alcoholic in recovery might wait until he earns his five-year sobriety chip to have a big party to celebrate, but it was the impulse to put down his drink in the first place that started it all, followed by his ability to listen to that impulse and push the glass away. And then his ability to make that same choice again the next day. And the next. None of us will ever make it to the five-year-chip-type moments without all the small victories along the way, so let's celebrate more of them.

The small wins are the real ones, as far as I'm concerned, because they're the ones that are sustainable. We can't expect to have big moments every day, but we can have small ones whenever we want them. And those small ones can build on each other, become habits, and lead to real, lasting transformation. That's why I look at every moment as an opportunity to make it count. Of course, making a moment count still takes effort, so when it works—whether it's realizing something about yourself or taking a small step to correct something you're unhappy about, or whatever it is—choose to give yourself credit for it. You need to do this for yourself as well as for the people around you. After all, how can you give someone else a break when you can't give one to yourself?

CHOOSE TRUST

One of the reasons why it's important to celebrate when we can is that choosing the light can be unpredictable. Not every moment is going to be a happy one. Not every effort you make is going to feel good.

One of the most difficult, but also the most profound, things we can do in this life is to choose to trust that there is light in *every* circumstance. A lot of people trust in the goodness they can see. They give when it's easy. They love when it feels good. But what about all the other times? Those are the times when light is needed the most.

When people ask me why I take chances in my life—take chances on people, take chances in my career, take chances by moving to a new city, take chances in anything—I always have the same answer: I can take chances because I trust. I trust that there's light, even when I can't see it. I trust the goodness in the world, despite all the chaos we see. I trust that there's good in every moment, even in the darkest times. That's because I believe darkness is temporary. But light is infinite.

This is a choice I make daily, because for me there's no other place to live than in the light. I give because I *am* a giver. I love because I am love. Light is what I want to be surrounded by in my life, and I don't believe that you can get there with hope alone. Hope can be paralyzing because it allows us to say, "I hope that things will get better, and I'll sit here and wait until they do." But that's not enough. Instead, trust that your actions will make things better. Choose not to wait any longer, and instead walk toward the light. Choose to run toward it even when you can't see it. Choose to trust that it's there and that you'll find it, if you just keep trying.

It makes me think of a quote I once read by Jay-Z. When he was starting out his career, he and his then business partners went to label after label and kept getting shut down, time and time again. It must have been difficult, but that didn't stop them. Instead, they chose to start their own label, and look what happened as a result. As Jay-Z explained at the 2010 Forbes 400 Summit, "The genius thing that we did was we didn't give up."[1]

He said something similar a few years later after his relationship with Beyoncé went through a very painful, and very public, rocky patch. But, again, they kept trying, trusting that their efforts were worth it even when things were at their darkest. "Most humans . . . we're not willing to put ourselves through that," Jay-Z explained. "Most people give up."[2]

But not the Carters. "We had to get to the point of 'OK, tear this down and let's start from the beginning. It's hard. Remember . . . I'm from Marcy Projects. I've been shot at. But nothing is harder than this. By far. I'm telling you, it's the hardest thing I've ever done."

Love often is that way. Love may be the hardest thing we ever choose. And yet imagine what life would be without it.

CHOOSE TO GIVE YOUR HEART MORE CREDIT

There are lots of reasons why someone might give up on love or turn a blind eye toward suffering, but when you strip them back, I think at the root of all the reasons is one common factor: fear. It's fear that allows us to walk past someone who's suffering, that causes us to look away from what's wrong with the world, what's wrong in our relationship, and what's wrong with ourselves. Fear that we'll be hurt and that we won't be strong enough to bear it. Fear that we're not powerful enough to do anything about it. Fear that we'll be judged or that we'll do the wrong thing.

And maybe we will. And maybe, so what? If I were to leave you with just one thought for the end of this book, it would be this: Start giving your heart more credit. Stop guarding it, because it doesn't need that from you. Your heart is strong, and it can fight for itself. So let it fight.

It's going to get messy sometimes. And ugly. And sad. And the world can be harsh and people can be difficult. And that's why we all need to get our hearts into fighting shape, so they can be ready for all of it. You've probably heard the old saying that life is a marathon, not a sprint. Well it is, if we're lucky, and marathons take practice and conditioning. That's why we started off with micro-gestures. They are a way of exercising your heart, just a little at first, and then more and more over time. The more you exercise your heart, the more you'll get to know its strength. That's when you'll begin to understand that your heart can bear a lot more than you've been asking it to. You don't need to protect it; you need to use it because that's what it's there for. It wants to be used.

We can come to understand this when we start listening to our hearts in silence. That's where the truth can be found, and we can draw strength from the truth in our hearts. Among the truths I want to leave you with are these:

- ♥ We all deserve to have a good life and to know that we're loved—no matter who we are, no matter where we come from, no matter what.

- ♥ We all suffer in one way or another, but it's our blindness to other people's suffering that compounds our own.

- ♥ There are people out there whose blessings are dependent on our generosity. Things are given to us so that we can become distributors, yet so many of us hoard what we have, feel like we don't have enough to share, refuse to help. That means we are hoarding our blessings.

- ♥ Those blessings are the light we've been given by God, or the Universe, or whatever you choose to call it. When we don't distribute the light we've been given, it goes out.

- ♥ Wherever you find suffering, you'll also find hope. Wherever you find suffering, you'll also find healing. That's where you come in. That's where you can truly make a difference in the world. You can fulfill someone's hope, contribute to someone's healing. Things can get better. You can make them better in your way.

- ♥ By helping to heal others, you can start to heal yourself. And don't we all need a bit of healing?

As one last exercise for your heart, go back through this book and look at all the different "Why I Give a F❤ck" quotes that appear in each chapter. When I started writing this book, I began asking different people, from different professions, backgrounds, and age groups, what made them care about others, what made them choose to give, or in short, what made them give a f❤ck about something other than themselves. I was surprised to learn just how many different answers there were to this question. Every single person I asked had a very different and very personal response.

So now it's your turn. Ask yourself: *Why do I give a f❤ck?*

And keep on asking yourself that question. Your answer may change or evolve over time. Or you may have one single answer that serves as your fixed and guiding light throughout the whole of your life. Either way, take some time to understand your reason and then let that reason inform your actions.

CHOOSE LOVE

We all have the capacity to make things better for one another and for ourselves if we choose to focus on love and bring it into every encounter that we can. If we can do this together, then we can have a better world.

There's nothing more motivating or sustaining than seeing how the choice to bring forward even just a little bit of love can change someone's life. When I first started LOM, we would do what we called food drive-bys—we picked up food from organic restaurants and grocery stores at midnight after they closed, packaged it into single-meal servings, and took it to Skid Row, where we'd drive around distributing it from the windows of our car at two in the morning. That's how I met Kevin. We'd see him regularly on our visits. He didn't say a lot, but he'd always greet us with a smile and a nonchalant, "Oh, you girls are back again?"

I'd been feeding Kevin for about a year when one day, without warning, he just wasn't there anymore. Week after week I'd look for him to no avail. I'd gotten attached to him by then, so I asked around about the man who didn't speak much, but no one knew what had happened to him or where he'd gone.

After a while, I no longer expected to see Kevin on our visits to Skid Row, but I never stopped wondering about him. Then one day, another full year later, he just showed up again on the corner of Sixth Street and Crocker, where we'd set up a table to hand out food. But this time he didn't want anything from us. He came to ask if he could help. He wanted to volunteer.

I was stunned when I saw him. He looked so handsome with his new clothes and haircut. He also had a noticeable air of confidence about him. I threw my arms around his neck and asked, "Kevin, where have you been?"

"I've been busy changing," he said with a little laugh.

I stepped back from him so I could see his face. I knew he was telling the truth. "What changed you?" I asked him.

"You girls changed me," he said. "You all coming here every morning at two to bring me food. It made me want to change, so I prayed to God every day that I saw you. I told Him that if he gave me a second chance, I would use it to repay you."

And that's what Kevin did. He got himself into a culinary program and became a chef. He then got a job at a well-known restaurant and moved into a new home. Now, in his spare time, he helps us make food for people who are living as he once did.

"When I'd wake up at two a.m. and see you down here feeding people, I thought there must be something wrong with you," Kevin laughed as he explained it all to me. "But then I realized that you didn't have an agenda. You just did it out of love. You loved me enough to do that for me when I didn't love myself. It made me want to change. It made me want to heal. It made me want more out of my life."

I feel like even one story like Kevin's is inspiration enough for any of us, but you can have hundreds of them to draw from if you keep your heart open and dare to try. Because your energy affects others. Because your love can make a difference. You may not even realize how much. So go distribute what you have to give. Go practice Love Without Reason.

And never, ever stop.

Appendix

MENU OF MICRO-GESTURES

What follows is a catalog of different ways you can think about giving, caring, sharing, and Loving Without Reason. These are all fairly simple things that just about anyone can do in various aspects of their life. You can pick and choose the ones that suit you best or try them all. You might also want to sit down with your tribe—your family, your children, your roommates, your friends—and talk about how you can bring more love and caring into the world together. You can even use this section as inspiration to create your own menu of caring gestures (and consider posting about them to inspire others using #microgestures).

Remember that this isn't about keeping score or doing the "right" thing. This is about exercising your heart for your own sake as well as others and attempting to bring a little bit more love into the world. It's true that some people will be more receptive to your gestures than others will be, and that some gestures will be more effective than others. And that's just the way things go. Try to detach yourself from the outcome and focus on your intention to Love Without Reason. Micro-gestures are about putting positive energy out there and then just letting it flow.

Pay Attention

Pick a time when you're out of the house, when you can practice being intentional about noticing people and finding ways to connect. This simply means making an effort to pay attention to the people around you instead of focusing on what's happening in your own head. You might do this while you're at the grocery store by looking around and noticing if someone could use help reaching an item on a high shelf or distracting an active or unhappy child. You might do it at work when you're taking a break by making a point of thanking someone for the work she's done that week or telling someone how much you like his outfit. Paying attention like this is a great thing to create a habit around. If you make a point of doing it every time you're at the grocery store, for example, then your powers of attention will start to kick in automatically when you're in that setting.

Servers and Cashiers

The next time you're in line for coffee or sitting in a restaurant or cafe, take note of the person serving you. People in service jobs are often looked past or treated rudely, so use it as an opportunity to practice being mindful, intentional, and generous. Start by putting away your phone so you can look at the person, make eye contact if possible, and notice his mood. Be intentional about acknowledging the person's presence by saying hello and maybe making a bit of small talk (a joke or compliment is always a good bet). And be generous with your thank-yous and even your tips. I often leave a short note on the check, just a line or two of thanks, along with my tip, especially if the server did or said something to brighten my day or looks like he could use a pick-me-up.

The Roll-Up

This one is about simply showing up for people. I had a good friend who'd just gone through a painful breakup. Rather than wait for her to reach out to us, a mutual friend and I got in the car, drove to where she lived, and rolled up to her house. We could have called first, but I think it's best to just show up if someone is really hurting, because let's face it: a lot of times people in pain won't know how to reach out or will try to push you away, even if that's not what they really need or want. If she'd asked us to leave when we got there (which she didn't—she cried when she saw us because she was so touched), we still would have conveyed to her how much she meant to us just by showing up.

And before you protest—"But what if someone just wants to be left alone!"—I once read similar advice from a bereavement counselor. He said that people always ask him what to do or say when someone has died, so his advice: make some food, write a condolence card and include any reheating instructions in the envelope, and then just show up at the person's home. Knock on the door, and if the person answers, tell him you're not there to bother him; you just want to make sure he has something good for dinner and that he knows you're there to help out however you can. And if he doesn't answer the door, leave the dish on the doorstep with your note.

I thought that was a great idea, but the best part of the counselor's advice was this: someone in mourning is already overwhelmed, so don't ask first; just do it.

Pick the Wallflowers

When you're at a party or work event, there's almost always someone who's standing in the corner looking awkward and alone. I know because I was that person at one point in my life at practically every party. A micro-gesture can be making an effort to draw out that person and helping her to feel comfortable. I often use a bit of humor to break through. You can try something like:

"Hey, do you like anyone in this room yet? Because I'm not so sure myself."

"Do you feel like this overpriced food is terrible too?"

"What brought you here? 'Cause I came to make friends but that's not happening."

Then see if the conversation flows from there. It doesn't even have to be a long one. Never underestimate the value of simply helping someone feel seen and accepted, if only for a moment. These are things that, deep down, all of us are looking for in this world.

Be Someone's Eyes

Be My Eyes is an organization that helps blind and low-vision people lead more independent lives by connecting them with what they call "micro-volunteers" to assist with everyday tasks. To become a micro-volunteer, all you have to do is download the free mobile app and wait for a call. When someone needs help, you'll be connected to a live video chat. The person on the other end might want help choosing a T-shirt to match his outfit. Or maybe she will point her phone at a package of food and ask you to read the expiration date. Whatever it is, it generally takes only a few minutes and you can do it from wherever you and your smartphone happen to be.

Settings allow you to choose what language(s) you speak and your local time zone so you won't receive calls in the middle of the night. And if you're busy when the call comes in, all you have to do is hit decline and another volunteer will handle it. It's that simple. Helping someone out literally couldn't be easier.

Take People for Treats

This is a great thing to do for someone who doesn't have a lot of extra cash, but it's also a nice way to say "thank you" or "I was thinking about you" to just about anyone. After all, everyone loves a treat, but I've found that the real treat is in the choice. So say to someone: "I feel like treating you. What would you like?" If the person is unsure, offer some suggestions: "Ice cream, a donut, a kombucha, a gossip magazine?" There was a guy who would hang out in front of my local Starbucks, who had a place to live and enough to eat, but because he was on public assistance, he never had enough cash left over at the end of the month to buy anything extra. I never would have guessed it of something so simple, but tea was the biggest treat for him. So much so that he would wait outside the shop hoping someone would notice him and offer him one, which is what I did. It was such a simple way to make someone's day.

Put Together Care Packages
If we think about it, a lot of us tend to get offered freebies on a pretty regular basis—samples from stores, trial sizes of new products, toiletries at hotels. If they're not something we like or use, we often turn them down. Instead, think about collecting these things to distribute to those who could use them. Not just the homeless, but seniors or people living paycheck to paycheck might love to get these things from you.

For example, I've found that hygiene and beauty products are among the first things people give up when they're short on cash, so every time I stay at a hotel, I take everything they have to offer. If housekeeping is willing, I might even collect some extras. And then, periodically, I'll put together care packages filled with mini toothpastes, shampoos, mouthwashes, lotions, etc. I put the items in tote bags (especially if I have freebies of those on hand) so they're easy to carry, or a gift bag to make it feel a bit more special. Then I give them away to whoever could use them.

Care for the Caretakers
We all know people who spend a lot of time caring for others. Maybe for someone they love who is ill or injured. Maybe for a newborn who requires all their focus and energy at the moment. Maybe they are doing their best to help their families or their communities through an emergency. When you see someone in a situation that leaves them little or no time for themselves, think about what you can do to care for them and make their caretaking duties just a little bit easier.

You could take the person a meal or give a gift certificate to have dinner or groceries delivered. You could spend the day with the caretaker's child or sick relative so that he or she can get out of the house for a while. You could offer to run errands for the person. If it's not obvious what you can do to help, then ask: "I can see that you do so much to care for others. What can I do to make things a little easier for you?"

"How About You?"

If you're getting up to get yourself coffee or tea at the office, make it a practice to ask the people near you if they want one too. (Assuming they're not focused intently on their work; be mindful not to interrupt.) Do the same if you're ordering food or picking it up on the way to someone's house or some kind of gathering. Don't assume that people have thought ahead or will take care of themselves. If I'm getting something for myself, I always ask if I can get others something too. It's a small, thoughtful gesture that helps build a sense of community and caring.

Be a Mentor

Think back to what it was like when you were young and trying to figure out what you wanted to do with your life. What made a difference for you as you chose a path or embarked on a career? Often, it was a person who told you that you had talent at something, gave you a chance at a job or internship, or listened and offered advice as you worked through your options. Now that you have some real-world experience of your own, you can be that same kind of resource for a young person by becoming a mentor. You can do this through a formal organization or informally, with a child you know in your neighborhood. The point is to offer young people some perspective and resources they wouldn't otherwise have as they figure out how they are going to make their own way in the world.

Sponsor a Classroom

Even if you don't have children, everyone lives near a school. Get to know a local teacher and ask what you can provide the teacher's classroom that will be of use. This could come in the form of school supplies (because, sadly, many teachers have to reach into their own pockets to purchase the things their student's need to learn) or items for the kids themselves. Most teachers will know who among their classroom might be struggling at home and could use some extra help with lunches, clothing, toiletries, or other necessities.

Connect with Local Nonprofits You Admire

Checks are great, but also consider what else you might be able to offer an organization that supports your community, especially if it's something that will foster a connection with the people the organization serves. If you have the skills, you could teach art classes or meditation at a local domestic violence shelter. A coffee shop owner could offer neighborhood kids a free and safe place to get together and do their homework after school. Do an inventory of the skills you have and then think creatively about how you might be able to offer them to different groups in need.

It's also a great idea to do something to raise money for an organization you admire. People I know have sold their excess or unneeded belongings on eBay or at a yard sale so they could donate the profits to a good cause. Or they've thrown parties or hosted events, promising half the proceeds to a cause they care about. These are ways to give that don't require you to have a lot of money to spare.

"Just Because" Celebrations

A night out at the movies. A favorite meal prepared at home. A note of appreciation. Just because someone is a regular in your life story doesn't mean that person knows you think of him or her as a star. So do something to make the people who are important to you *feel* important, like taking them out on the town or telling them how you feel—not because they've done something special for you lately, but just because they *are* special to you. Sometimes the people we rely on the most are the ones we most take for granted. Once a month—you can even set a reminder on your calendar app—find a way to show the people you care about the most just how important they are to you.

Check-Ins

If you know someone who has been ill or gone through a rough time lately, or even if you just haven't talked to someone in a while, drop that person a note or send a text to check in: "I've been thinking about you and wanted to know how you're doing." It's a simple, easy, and cheap way to let someone know that you care and that you're there if he or she needs you.

"How About a Coffee?"

Coffee is a $5 gift that you can give to just about anyone. Acquaintances. People in your office. Someone on the street. A friend once drove into a parking lot on a winter day and could tell that the attendant in the booth was cold. So as she was leaving the lot, she asked if she could bring him back a coffee. He was so grateful, saying it was "exactly what I needed," but he wasn't allowed to leave the booth so he wouldn't have been able to get it himself. It was such a simple way to perk up someone's day.

Surprise a Stranger

If you have some extra cash in your pocket, think about using it to make someone's day for no reason at all. If you're at a drive-through or in line for coffee, you can give the cashier a little bit extra to pay for the person behind you. Or, if you're at a restaurant and see someone dining alone, ask the server to bring you the person's check. People remember gestures like this and are genuinely touched by them. It's also a great way to inspire people to pay it forward.

Tidying Up

Getting rid of excess stuff can be really satisfying, so set aside a weekend or part of your next vacation to do a purge of all the things you don't need or want anymore. But instead of throwing them away, set aside anything that's in good shape (this is important; giving people your broken-down junk doesn't feel like a gift) and that someone else might be able to use. Kitchen items, clothing, packaged foods, toys your kids have outgrown, books you've already read, exercise or recreational equipment you don't use anymore—all these things could be welcome gifts for someone else. Take them to a local donation center or put an ad on Craigslist or Nextdoor offering what you have for free to whoever is willing to come and get it. You might even meet some new neighbors that way too!

Redirect an Uncomfortable Conversation

Maybe there's someone in a group conversation who looks like he feels left out. Or maybe the conversation has taken a negative turn and someone is being criticized or put down. Take notice and make an effort to infuse some inclusiveness and positivity into the moment. You might ask the left-out person a direct question or counter a negative remark with your own positive spin. The main thing is not to ignore the discomfort, and instead make an effort to change the dynamic for the better.

More Thank Yous

People do nice things for us all the time, but we don't always notice. In fact, the more common the task, the less likely we are to pay attention. I think that's a shame. If you tweak your perspective a bit and actively look for opportunities to say thank you, I bet you'll find they happen all the time. Is it your husband's job to take out the trash? Say thank you when you see him do it, even if it's something he does every week. (After all, aren't you glad you don't have to do it?) How about the person who cleans your desk at work? Tell her how glad you are to see her or leave her a thank-you note if she usually comes after hours.

Ever thanked the person who delivers your mail? Now's a good time if you haven't, or even if you have. Just because it's someone's job doesn't mean that person doesn't deserve some credit for doing it and doing it well.

Lend an Ear

There are a lot of people out there, whether they're strangers or people we know well, who could really use a chance to unload and/or connect. Maybe someone is feeling lonely and could use a chat. Maybe someone is having a hard time at home and could use someone impartial to talk to about it. Maybe someone's kid is driving him crazy and he could use a chance to unload so he doesn't take it out on the kid directly. Maybe someone has a problem she just needs to talk through. If we're paying attention, we'll likely pick up on the signals that someone would like to talk in all sorts of situations—a stranger on the bus, a coworker who hasn't been herself, our own friend or family member who has been uncharacteristically withdrawn. Instead of ignoring the signs or cutting people off, offer to listen. And then really do it. Don't check your texts. Don't look over the person's shoulder. Don't interrupt or talk about yourself. Instead, focus your full attention on the other person, and let him or her use you as a sounding board. It's a gift people are usually so very thankful for.

Check the Weather

Bad weather is one of those little annoyances in life that can really ruin someone's day. But it can also be an opportunity to make someone's day if you're intentional about it. The next time you see someone who has gotten caught in the rain without an umbrella, offer to share yours and walk the person to wherever he or she needs to go. Or if you're shoveling out your car after a heavy snow, look around and see if a few of your neighbors could use some help with their own cars.

When All Else Fails, Ask

Too often we choose not to reach out to someone or try to help because we think, or we're afraid, that the person doesn't want us to. We think we're being presumptuous. We worry that we'll bother the person, or worse, offend him or her. My answer in moments like these is almost always the same: if you're not sure what to do, don't turn away—just ask.

"I get the feeling that you're hurting, and I'm so sorry about that. Is there anything I can do?"

"I know your breakup is a sensitive issue, but I'd love to help if I can—whatever that means to you."

e merge into traffic in front of you.

nber of your family has a chore to do, offer to do it yourself
him or her a break.

ffort to articulate your feelings with the people you care
ng "I love you" or telling them how happy you are to see
u're at a loss for words, don't shut down—just take a mo-
d them.

see someone who hangs out regularly in front of a place
shop, acknowledge the person and say: "I see you every time
e, and I would love to know your name so next time I can

es of water and granola bars in your car to distribute when
nter someone in need.

hone away and listen to someone, giving that person your
attention.

hugger and offer hugs wherever you can!

"I don't want to bother y
I'm here for you when and

Don't let a sensitive or aw
out and ask the person wha
or is too shut down, to acce
sometimes that's all a person
what he or she is going thro

Quick Micro-Gestures

So many micro-gestures take
an effort to do them, and thr
The following ideas are the qu
moments in your day.

- Next time you're at a
  reception, be the one

- Give up your seat on
  could use it.

- Help someone who is

- Pick up the tab for lun

- When you get in line a
  behind you go first if y

- Always smile at or say h
  a walk.

- Ask someone, "How's y

- Instead of staring silent
  elevator, pick out someo
  offer a compliment.

- Next time you're enterir
  looking behind you and

- Let someo

- When a me
  just to give

- Make an
  about, say
  them. If y
  ment to fi

- When you
  where you
  I come he
  say hello."

- Keep bott
  you encou

- Put your
  undivided

- Become a

Notes

Introduction: Why I Give a F♥ck

1. Martin Luther King, Jr., "'The Three Dimensions of a Complete Life,' Sermon Delivered at the Unitarian Church of Germantown," *The Papers of Martin Luther King, Jr., Volume V: Threshold of a New Decade, January 1959–December 1960*. Edited by Clayborne Carson, Tenisha Armstrong, Susan Carson, Adrienne Clay, and Kieran Taylor (University of California Press, 1992).

2. Gwen Costello, *Spiritual Gems from Mother Teresa* (Twenty-Third Publications, 2008).

Chapter 1: How Giving a F♥ck Can Change Your Life

1. Paulo Coelho, *The Alchemist* (HarperCollins, 2015).

2. Laura Vozzella and Emily Guskin, "In Virginia, a State of Political Separation: Most Clinton Voters Don't Know Any Trump Voters, and Vice Versa," *The Washington Post* (September 14, 2016).

3. Derek Thompson, "Everybody's in a Bubble, and That's a Problem," *The Atlantic* (January 25, 2017).

4. "Empathy: College Students Don't Have as Much as They Used To," *Michigan News*, University of Michigan (May 27, 2010).

5. Dennis Thompson, "More Americans Suffering from Stress, Anxiety and Depression, Study Finds," CBSNews.com (April 17, 2017).

6. Douglas Nemecek, MD, MBA, "2018 Cigna U.S. Loneliness Index" (May 2018), multivu.com/players/English/8294451-cigna-us -loneliness-survey/docs/IndexReport_1524069371598-173525450.pdf.

7. The Times Editorial Board, "Los Angeles' Homelessness Crisis Is a National Disgrace," *The Los Angeles Times* (February 25, 2018).

8. "'There's Something Terribly Wrong': Why More Americans Are Dying in Middle Age," Advisory Board (December 2, 2019), advisory.com /daily-briefing/2019/12/02/middle-age-death.

Chapter 2: Start with a Reset

1. Foundation for Inner Peace, *A Course in Miracles: Combined Volume*, 2nd edition (Viking, 1996).

2. Khalil Gibran, *The Prophet* (Rajpal & Sons, 2012).

3. Alisha Coleman-Jensen, et al., "Household Food Security in the United States in 2018," U.S. Department of Agriculture Economic Research Service.

4. Serusha Govender, "These Countries Waste Enough Food to Feed the Planet," *The Daily Meal* (August 6, 2014).

5. Oliver Milman, "Americans Waste 150,000 Tons of Food Each Day— Equal to a Pound Per Person," *The Guardian* (April 18, 2018).

6. Beverly Engel, LMFT, "When Did 'Victim' Become a Bad Word?: Why Do We Despise Weakness in Ourselves and Others?" *Psychology Today* (April 9, 2015).

7. Dennis McCarty, et al., "Alcoholism, Drug Abuse, and the Homeless," *American Psychologist* 46, no. 11 (November 1991): 1139–1148.

Chapter 3: Micro-gestures Will Change the World

1. Mother Teresa, *No Greater Love* (New World Library, 2002).

Chapter 4: The Energy Exchange

1. Fred Rogers, *The World According to Mister Rogers: Important Things to Remember* (Hachette Books, 2003).

Chapter 5: Lessons from Skid Row

1. Robert L. Perkins, *Works of Love* (Mercer University Press, 1999).

2. Utpal Dholakia, PhD, "Why People Who Have Less Give More," *Psychology Today* (November 20, 2017).

3. Colby Itkowitz, "The Science Behind Why You Shouldn't Stop Giving Thanks After Thanksgiving," *The Washington Post* (November 24, 2016).

4. Paulo Coelho, "What if the Universe Conspired in Your Favor?" *Oprah's SuperSoul Conversations* (August 9, 2017).

5. Partnership for Los Angeles Schools, "107th Street Elementary Joins the Partnership: A Case Study" (July 2017).

Chapter 6: Love Is a Discipline . . . and a Steeping

1. Toni Morrison, *Beloved* (Knopf Doubleday Publishing Group, 2007).

Chapter 7: When Love Is Labor

1. James Baldwin, *The Fire Next Time* (Knopf Doubleday Publishing Group, 2013).

2. Hara Estroff Marano, "Our Brain's Negative Bias," *Psychology Today* (June 20, 2003).

3. Micah Fitzerman-Blue and Noah Harpster, *A Beautiful Day in the Neighborhood*, directed by Marielle Heller, 2019.

4. Maxwell King, *The Good Neighbor: The Life and Work of Fred Rogers* (Abrams, 2018).

Chapter 8: Reset with Your Tribe

1. Mary Lutyens, *The Life and Death of Krishnamurti* (Random House, 2012).

Chapter 9: Keep Choosing the Light

1. Taylor Locke, "Jay Z Says This Is the 'Genius Thing' He Did When Starting Out in the Music Business," CNBC.com (October 18, 2019), cnbc.com/2019/10/18/jay-z-the-genius-thing-i-did-starting-out-in-music-business.html.

2. Cady Lang, "Jay-Z Discusses How His Marriage to Beyoncé Wasn't Built on '100 Percent Truth,'" *Time* (July 11, 2017), time.com/4852858/jay-z-beyonce-infidelity-marriage/.

Acknowledgments

First, I want to thank the people who have loved and supported me, and whom I have had the honor of loving throughout most, if not all, of my life: my dad, James Ellis; my seven siblings—Treviane, Deaza, Railyne, Kalieve, Kaiden, Shaheed, and Ricco—and my best friend since we were babies, Jamila Brown.

A special thanks to my Lunch On Me family—Venus Nari, Shaianne Johnson, Emily Tausaga, Matthew Rivers, and Ash Level—without whom none of this would be possible. And to our extended family of volunteers, who show up for us every week, as well as the Soulful Publicist, Tanya Khani, who does a fantastic job of making sure people know who we are and what we do.

Much gratitude to the generous souls whose support and sponsorship has made our work possible, including Elyse Hook at Whole Foods; Fusako Phares, treasurer at Phantasos; Steven Mikula at Sprouts; Rich Bertrand at Revive; Jeffrey Young at The New York Coffee Festival; Assaad Benabid at Faema; photographer Madgalena Wosinska; Rachel Krupa at The Goods Mart; baker extraordinaire Christina Lindh; Ravi Prakash at The Ravi Prakash Foundation; and Lizy Hoeffer.

And a heartfelt thanks to all the friends and supporters who have walked with me on this journey: Tanya "Sugar Dumpling" Brooks, Shamen Durek, Elena Santillo Valencia, Tragik (a.k.a. Florencia Garcia Carcagno), Meg Hairell, Amber and Ashton Whittington, Chalon, Simone Southwell, Nema Etebar, Tal Rabinowitz, and Priscilla Castro-Preciado.

When it comes to this book, I have to start by thanking Dr. Will Cole, who was the first to say to me, "You have a book inside you." He then connected me to Heather Jackson, who is both a wonderful person and a wonderful agent, all at once.

Thanks to my MindBodyGreen family—including Colleen Wachob, Jason Wachob, Olessa Pindall, Adaeza Elechi, and Andreas Von Scheele—for being so supportive and for being the first to encourage me to speak publicly about our work at Lunch On Me.

If it hadn't been for that first speech at an MBG event, I never would have met my dear friend Danielle "Chef" Shine. She was the one who connected me to Christa Bourg, who helped me write this book. Christa, I've been so blessed to get to know you and embark on this journey. Thank you for all that you've done, professionally, emotionally, and energetically. Your love, effort, and care is beyond measure. The book has been such a milestone, but gaining a friendship with you supersedes it.

And, of course, thanks to Haven Iverson and the entire team at Sounds True, who helped turn this crazy idea into a reality.

Finally, a heartfelt thanks to my street family on Skid Row for all the love and inspiration they provide me every day, including Walter, Montgomery, Scotty, Ms. Brenda, Kevin, Pegasus, Meeka, Fiji, Gabe, Delilah, Aiz, Janet, Rose, Peaches, Asher, Gregory, Nancy, Pepper, and Big Joe.

About the Author

LaRayia Gaston is the founder and executive director of Lunch On Me (lunchonme.org), a nonprofit dedicated to ending starvation by redirecting waste and providing opportunities to enrich the mind, body, and spirit of the nation's homeless communities. In its first three years of service, LOM served a quarter of a million plant-based meals to people in need in California, Texas, New York, Florida, Michigan, and Hawaii. In 2019, the organization expanded its programs by opening La Bodega, a vegan café and 99-cent store in the Westlake neighborhood of Los Angeles that offers healthy, organic food at budget prices for the city's underserved communities.

To promote Lunch On Me and its mission to Love Without Reason, Gaston has become a regular public speaker and guest on national radio shows, podcasts, and television shows, including *Good Morning America* and *The Doctors*. She recently became involved in documentary filmmaking and is currently working on a film called *43 Days on Skid Row*. The title comes from the amount of time she spent living among Skid Row's residents so that she could offer a true picture of what life is like in one of America's largest homeless communities.

Prior to starting Lunch On Me, Gaston worked as a model, actress, coffee shop owner, and designer for her own fashion brand, Apule Town (apuletown.com). She currently lives in Los Angeles with her two dogs, Nugget and Mali.

About Sounds True

Sounds True is a multimedia publisher whose mission is to inspire and support personal transformation and spiritual awakening. Founded in 1985 and located in Boulder, Colorado, we work with many of the leading spiritual teachers, thinkers, healers, and visionary artists of our time. We strive with every title to preserve the essential "living wisdom" of the author or artist. It is our goal to create products that not only provide information to a reader or listener but also embody the quality of a wisdom transmission.

For those seeking genuine transformation, Sounds True is your trusted partner. At SoundsTrue.com you will find a wealth of free resources to support your journey, including exclusive weekly audio interviews, free downloads, interactive learning tools, and other special savings on all our titles.

To learn more, please visit SoundsTrue.com/freegifts or call us tollfree at 800.333.9185.

"I don't want to bother you or get in your way, but I want you to know that I'm here for you when and if you need anything."

Don't let a sensitive or awkward situation be an excuse not to try. Just reach out and ask the person what you can do. Even if he or she is hurting too much, or is too shut down, to accept your gesture, it will still register as caring. And sometimes that's all a person really needs: to know that someone out there sees what he or she is going through and cares enough to offer a helping hand.

Quick Micro-Gestures

So many micro-gestures take hardly any time or energy. You just have to make an effort to do them, and through your effort they'll get easier to do every day! The following ideas are the quickest and simplest ways to bring LWR into more moments in your day.

- ♥ Next time you're at an awkward dinner party, conference, or wedding reception, be the one to say hi first and introduce yourself.

- ♥ Give up your seat on the bus or subway to someone who looks like he could use it.

- ♥ Help someone who is struggling with her packages or stroller.

- ♥ Pick up the tab for lunch for a friend or stranger just because.

- ♥ When you get in line at the grocery store or coffee shop, let the person behind you go first if you're not in a hurry.

- ♥ Always smile at or say hello to the people you pass when you're out for a walk.

- ♥ Ask someone, "How's your day going?" and really listen to the answer.

- ♥ Instead of staring silently ahead when you're awkwardly packed in an elevator, pick out someone who looks like she or he could use a lift and offer a compliment.

- ♥ Next time you're entering an elevator or a building, make a point of looking behind you and holding the door for anyone who's coming.

- ❤ Let someone merge into traffic in front of you.

- ❤ When a member of your family has a chore to do, offer to do it yourself just to give him or her a break.

- ❤ Make an effort to articulate your feelings with the people you care about, saying "I love you" or telling them how happy you are to see them. If you're at a loss for words, don't shut down—just take a moment to find them.

- ❤ When you see someone who hangs out regularly in front of a place where you shop, acknowledge the person and say: "I see you every time I come here, and I would love to know your name so next time I can say hello."

- ❤ Keep bottles of water and granola bars in your car to distribute when you encounter someone in need.

- ❤ Put your phone away and listen to someone, giving that person your undivided attention.

- ❤ Become a hugger and offer hugs wherever you can!